# THE ARMED FORCES
# PRAYER BOOK

PUBLISHED FOR

## THE ARMED FORCES DIVISION OF
## THE PROTESTANT EPISCOPAL CHURCH

BY

THE CHURCH PENSION FUND

20 Exchange Place · New York

1951

# PROTESTANT EPISCOPAL CHURCH
## IN THE UNITED STATES OF AMERICA

### OFFICE OF THE PRESIDING BISHOP
### 281 FOURTH AVENUE
### NEW YORK 10, N. Y.

#### THE RT. REV. HENRY K. SHERRILL, D.D.

June 5, 1951

This Prayer Book is sent by the Church to the men and women of the Armed Forces, with the assurance of the affection, the deep interest and the prayers of the Church people at home for God's blessing upon you. We follow all that you do and are with gratitude. May this book be a reminder of your dedication in Baptism to be Christ's faithful soldier and servant to your life's end. You will find these prayers, hymns and Bible readings a daily source of spiritual strength and courage.

HENRY K. SHERRILL
*Presiding Bishop*

The Protestant Episcopal Church in the United States of America

# Contents

# Contents

# An Order of Worship

## HYMN

The LORD is in his holy temple: let all the earth keep silence before him. *Hab. ii.* 20.

I was glad when they said unto me, We will go into the house of the LORD. *Psalm cxxii.* 1.

Let the words of my mouth, and the meditation of my heart, be alway acceptable in thy sight, O LORD, my strength and my redeemer. *Psalm xix.* 14.

O send out thy light and thy truth, that they may lead me, and bring me unto thy holy hill, and to thy dwelling. *Psalm xliii.* 3.

Grace be unto you, and peace, from God our Father, and from the Lord Jesus Christ. *Phil. i.* 2.

## PSALM

## SCRIPTURE LESSON

## HYMN

## APOSTLES' CREED

I believe in God the Father Almighty, Maker of heaven and earth:

And in Jesus Christ his only Son our Lord: Who was conceived by the Holy Ghost, Born of the Virgin Mary: Suffered under Pontius Pilate, Was crucified, dead, and buried: He descended into hell; The third day he rose again from the dead: He ascended into heaven, And sitteth on the right hand of God the

Father Almighty: From thence he shall come to judge the quick and the dead.

I believe in the Holy Ghost: The holy Catholic Church; The Communion of Saints: The Forgiveness of sins: The Resurrection of the body: And the Life everlasting. Amen.

> The Lord be with you.
> *Answer.* And with thy spirit.
> *Minister.* Let us pray.

### A Confession

O Almighty Father, Lord of heaven and earth, we confess that we have sinned against thee in thought, word, and deed. Have mercy upon us, O God, after thy great goodness; according to the multitude of thy mercies, do away our offences and cleanse us from our sins; for Jesus Christ's sake. Amen.

### Absolution

The Almighty and merciful Lord grant you Absolution and Remission of all your sins, true repentance, amendment of life, and the grace and consolation of his Holy Spirit. *Amen.*

## PRAYERS (to be chosen by the Minister)

### A General Thanksgiving

Almighty God, Father of all mercies, we, thine unworthy servants, do give thee most humble and hearty thanks for all thy goodness and loving-kindness to us, and to all men. We bless thee for our creation, preservation, and all the blessings of this life; but above all, for thine inestimable love in the redemption of the world by our Lord Jesus Christ; for the means of grace, and for the hope of glory. And, we beseech thee, give us that due sense of all thy mercies, that our hearts may be unfeignedly thankful; and that we show forth thy praise, not only with our lips, but in our lives, by giving up our selves to thy service, and by walking before thee in holiness and righteousness all our days; through Jesus Christ our Lord, to whom, with thee and the Holy Ghost, be all honour and glory, world without end. *Amen.*

Our Father, who art in heaven, Hallowed be thy Name. Thy kingdom come. Thy will be done, On earth as it is in heaven. Give us this day our daily bread. And forgive us our trespasses, As we forgive those who trespass against us. And lead us not into temptation, But deliver us from evil. For thine is the kingdom, and the power, and the glory, for ever and ever. Amen.

### 2 Cor. xiii. 14.

The grace of our Lord Jesus Christ, and the love of God, and the fellowship of the Holy Ghost, be with us all evermore. *Amen.*

## HYMN

## ADDRESS

The LORD bless us, and keep us. The LORD make his face to shine upon us, and be gracious unto us. The LORD lift up his countenance upon us, and give us peace, both now and evermore. *Amen.*

# The Order for

## The Administration of the Lord's Supper

### or

# Holy Communion

¶ *At the Communion-time the Holy Table shall have upon it a fair white linen cloth. And the Priest, standing reverently before the Holy Table, shall say the Lord's Prayer and the Collect following, the People kneeling; but the Lord's Prayer may be omitted at the discretion of the Priest.*

Our Father, who art in heaven, Hallowed be thy Name. Thy kingdom come. Thy will be done, On earth as it is heaven. Give us this day our daily bread. And forgive us our trespasses, As we forgive those who trespass against us. And lead us not into temptation, But deliver us from evil. Amen.

### The Collect.

Almighty God, unto whom all hearts are open, all desires known, and from whom no secrets are hid; Cleanse the thoughts of our hearts by the inspiration of thy Holy Spirit, that we may perfectly love thee, and worthily magnify thy holy Name; through Christ our Lord. *Amen.*

¶ *Then shall the Priest, turning to the People, rehearse distinctly The Ten Commandments; and the People, still kneeling, shall, after every Commandment, ask God mercy for their transgressions for the time past, and grace to keep the law for the time to come.*

¶ *And* NOTE, *That in rehearsing The Ten Commandments, the Priest may omit that part of the Commandment which is inset.*

¶ *The Decalogue may be omitted, provided it be said at least one Sunday in each month. But* NOTE, *That whenever it is omitted, the Priest shall say the Summary of the Law, beginning,* Hear what our Lord Jesus Christ saith.

5

# Holy Communion

### The Decalogue.

God spake these words, and said:
I am the LORD thy God; Thou shalt have none other gods but me.

*Lord, have mercy upon us, and incline our hearts to keep this law.*

Thou shalt not make to thyself any graven image, nor the likeness of any thing that is in heaven above, or in the earth beneath, or in the water under the earth; thou shalt not bow down to them, nor worship them;

for I the LORD thy God am a jealous God, and visit the sins of the fathers upon the children, unto the third and fourth generation of them that hate me; and show mercy unto thousands in them that love me and keep my commandments.

*Lord, have mercy upon us, and incline our hearts to keep this law.*

Thou shalt not take the Name of the LORD thy God in vain;

for the LORD will not hold him guiltless, that taketh his Name in vain.

*Lord, have mercy upon us, and incline our hearts to keep this law.*

Remember that thou keep holy the Sabbath-day.

Six days shalt thou labour, and do all that thou hast to do; but the seventh day is the Sabbath of the LORD thy God. In it thou shalt do no manner of work; thou, and thy son, and thy daughter, thy man-servant, and thy maid-servant, thy cattle, and the stranger that is within thy gates. For in six days the LORD made heaven and earth, the sea, and all that in them is, and rested the seventh day: wherefore the LORD blessed the seventh day, and hallowed it.

*Lord, have mercy upon us, and incline our hearts to keep this law.*

Honour thy father and thy mother;

that thy days may be long in the land which the LORD thy God giveth thee.

*Lord, have mercy upon us, and incline our hearts to keep this law.*

Thou shalt do no murder.

*Lord, have mercy upon us, and incline our hearts to keep this law.*

Thou shalt not commit adultery.

*Lord, have mercy upon us, and incline our hearts to keep this law.*

Thou shalt not steal.

*Lord, have mercy upon us, and incline our hearts to keep this law.*

Thou shalt not bear false witness against thy neighbour.

*Lord, have mercy upon us, and incline our hearts to keep this law.*

Thou shall not covet

thy neighbour's house, thou shalt not covet thy neighbour's wife, nor his servant, nor his maid, nor his ox, nor his ass, nor any thing that is his.

*Lord, have mercy upon us, and write all these thy laws in our hearts, we beseech thee.*

¶ *Then may the Priest say,*

Hear what our Lord Jesus Christ saith.

Thou shalt love the Lord thy God with all thy heart, and with all thy soul, and with all thy mind. This is the first and great commandment. And the second is like unto it; Thou shalt love thy neighbour as thyself. On these two commandments hang all the Law and the Prophets.

*¶ Here, if the Decalogue hath been omitted, shall be said,*

Lord, have mercy upon us.
*Christ, have mercy upon us.*
Lord, have mercy upon us.

*¶ Then the Priest may say,*

O Almighty Lord, and everlasting God, vouchsafe, we beseech thee, to direct, sanctify, and govern, both our hearts and bodies, in the ways of thy laws, and in the works of thy commandments; that, through thy most mighty protection, both here and ever, we may be preserved in body and soul; through our Lord and Saviour Jesus Christ. *Amen.*

*¶ Here shall be said,*

The Lord be with you.
*Answer.* And with thy spirit.
*Minister.* Let us pray.

*¶ Then shall the Priest say the Collect of the Day. And after the Collect the Minister appointed shall read the Epistle, first saying, The Epistle is written in the — Chapter of —, beginning at the — Verse. The Epistle ended, he shall say, Here endeth the Epistle.*

*¶ Here may be sung a Hymn or an Anthem.*

*¶ Then, all the People standing, the Minister appointed shall read the Gospel, first saying, The Holy Gospel is written in the — Chapter of —, beginning at the — Verse.*

*¶ Here shall be said,*

Glory be to thee, O Lord.

*¶ And after the Gospel may be said,*

Praise be to thee, O Christ.

*¶ Then shall be said the Creed commonly called the Nicene, or else the Apostles' Creed; but the Creed may be omitted, if it hath been said immediately before in Morning Prayer; Provided, That the Nicene Creed shall be said on Christmas Day, Easter Day, Ascension Day, Whitsunday, and Trinity Sunday.*

I believe in one God the Father Almighty, Maker of heaven and earth, And of all things visible and invisible:

And in one Lord Jesus Christ, the only-begotten Son of God; Begotten of his Father before all worlds, God of God, Light of Light, Very God of very God; Begotten, not made; Being of one substance with the Father; By whom all things were made: Who for us men and for our salvation came down from heaven, And was incarnate by the Holy Ghost of the Virgin Mary, And was made man: And was crucified also for us under Pontius Pilate; He suffered and was buried: And the third day he rose again according to the Scriptures: And ascended into heaven, And sitteth on the right hand of the Father: And he shall come again, with glory, to judge both the quick and the dead; Whose kingdom shall have no end.

And I believe in the Holy Ghost, The Lord, and Giver of Life, Who proceedeth from the Father and the Son; Who with the Father and the Son together is worshipped and glorified; Who spake by the Prophets: And I believe one Catholic and Apostolic Church: I acknowledge one Baptism for the remission of sins: And I look for the Resurrection of the dead: And the Life of the world to come. Amen.

*¶ Then shall be declared unto the People what Holy Days, or Fasting Days, are in the week following to be observed; and (if occasion be) shall Notice be given of the Communion, and of the Banns of Matrimony, and of other matters to be published.*

*¶ Here, or immediately after the Creed, may be said the Bidding Prayer, or other authorized prayers and intercessions.*

¶ *Then followeth the Sermon. After which, the Priest, when there is a Communion, shall return to the Holy Table, and begin the Offertory, saying one or more of these Sentences following, as he thinketh most convenient.*

Remember the words of the Lord Jesus, how he said, It is more blessed to give than to receive. *Acts* xx. 35.

Thine, O LORD, is the greatness, and the power, and the glory, and the victory, and the majesty: for all that is in the heaven and in the earth is thine; thine is the kingdom, O LORD, and thou art exalted as head above all. 1 *Chron.* xxix. 11.

All things come of thee, O LORD, and of thine own have we given thee. 1 *Chron.* xxix. 14.

¶ *And* NOTE, *That these Sentences may be used on any other occasion of Public Worship when the Offerings of the People are to be received.*

¶ *The Deacons, Church-wardens, or other fit persons appointed for that purpose, shall receive the Alms for the Poor, and other Offerings of the People, in a decent Basin to be provided by the Parish; and reverently bring it to the Priest, who shall humbly present and place it upon the Holy Table.*

¶ *And the Priest shall then offer, and shall place upon the Holy Table, the Bread and the Wine.*

¶ *And when the Alms and Oblations are being received and presented, there may be sung a Hymn, or an Offertory Anthem in the words of Holy Scripture or of the Book of Common Prayer, under the direction of the Priest.*

¶ *Here the Priest may ask the secret intercessions of the Congregation for any who have desired the prayers of the Church.*

¶ *Then shall the Priest say,*

Let us pray for the whole state of Christ's Church.

Almighty and everliving God, who by thy holy Apostle hast taught us to make prayers, and supplications, and to give thanks for all men; We humbly beseech thee most mercifully to accept our [*alms and*] oblations, and to receive these our prayers, which we offer unto thy Divine Majesty; beseeching thee to inspire continually the Universal Church with the spirit of truth, unity, and concord: And grant that all those who do confess thy holy Name may agree in the truth of thy holy Word, and live in unity and godly love.

We beseech thee also, so to direct and dispose the hearts of all Christian Rulers, that they may truly and impartially administer justice, to the punishment of wickedness and vice, and to the maintenance of thy true religion, and virtue.

Give grace, O heavenly Father, to all Bishops and other Ministers, that they may, both by their life and doctrine, set forth thy true and lively Word, and rightly and duly administer thy holy Sacraments.

And to all thy People give thy heavenly grace; and especially to this congregation here present; that, with meek heart and due reverence, they may hear, and receive thy holy Word; truly serving thee in holiness and righteousness all the days of their life.

And we most humbly beseech thee, of thy goodness, O Lord, to comfort and succour all those who, in this transitory life, are in trouble, sorrow, need, sickness, or any other adversity.

And we also bless thy holy Name for all thy servants departed this life in thy faith and fear; beseeching thee to grant them continual growth in thy love and service, and to give us grace so to follow their good examples, that with them we may be partakers of thy heavenly kingdom. Grant this, O Father, for Jesus Christ's sake, our only Mediator and Advocate. *Amen.*

¶ *Then shall the Priest say to those who come to receive the Holy Communion,*

Ye who do truly and earnestly repent you of your sins, and are in love and charity with your neighbours, and intend to lead a new life, following the commandments of God, and walking from henceforth in his holy ways; Draw near with faith, and take this holy Sacrament to your comfort; and make your humble confession to Almighty God, devoutly kneeling.

¶ *Then shall this General Confession be made, by the Priest and all those who are minded to receive the Holy Communion, humbly kneeling.*

Almighty God, Father of our Lord Jesus Christ, Maker of all things, Judge of all men; We acknowledge and bewail our manifold sins and wickedness, Which we, from time to time, most grievously have committed, By thought, word, and deed, Against thy Divine Majesty, Provoking most justly thy wrath and indignation against us. We do earnestly repent, And are heartily sorry for these our misdoings; The remembrance of them is grievous unto us; The burden of them is intolerable. Have mercy upon us, Have mercy upon us, most merciful Father; For thy Son our Lord Jesus Christ's sake, Forgive us all that is past; And grant that we may ever hereafter Serve and please thee In newness of life, To the honour and glory of thy Name; Through Jesus Christ our Lord. Amen.

¶ *Then shall the Priest (the Bishop if he be present) stand up, and turning to the People, say,*

Almighty God, our heavenly Father, who of his great mercy hath promised forgiveness of sins to all those who with hearty repentance and true faith turn unto him; Have mercy upon you; pardon and deliver you from all your sins; confirm and strengthen you in all goodness; and bring you to everlasting life; through Jesus Christ our Lord. *Amen.*

¶ *Then shall the Priest say,*

Hear what comfortable words our Saviour Christ saith unto all who truly turn to him.

Come unto me, all ye that travail and are heavy laden, and I will refresh you. *St. Matt.* xi. 28.

So God loved the world, that he gave his only-begotten Son, to the end that all that believe in him should not perish, but have everlasting life. *St. John* iii. 16.

Hear also what Saint Paul saith.

This is a true saying, and worthy of all men to be received, That Christ Jesus came into the world to save sinners. 1 *Tim.* i. 15.

Hear also what Saint John saith.

If any man sin, we have an Advocate with the Father, Jesus Christ the righteous; and he is the Propitiation for our sins. 1 *St. John* ii. 1, 2.

¶ *After which the Priest shall proceed, saying,*

Lift up your hearts.

*Answer.* We lift them up unto the Lord.

*Priest.* Let us give thanks unto our Lord God.

*Answer.* It is meet and right so to do.

¶ *Then shall the Priest turn to the Holy Table, and say,*

It is very meet, right, and our bounden duty, that we should at all times, and in all places, give thanks unto thee, O Lord, Holy Father, Almighty, Everlasting God.

¶ *Here shall follow the Proper Preface, according to the time, if there be any specially appointed; or else immediately shall be said or sung by the Priest,*

Therefore with Angels and Archangels, and with all the company of heaven, we laud and magnify thy glorious Name; evermore praising thee, and saying,

HOLY, HOLY, HOLY, Lord    ¶ *Priest and People.*
God of hosts, Heaven and earth are
full of thy glory: Glory be to thee, O Lord Most High.
Amen.

## PROPER PREFACES

### CHRISTMAS

¶ *Upon Christmas Day, and seven days after.*

Because thou didst give Jesus Christ, thine only Son, to be born as at this time for us; who, by the operation of the Holy Ghost, was made very man, of the substance of the Virgin Mary his mother; and that without spot of sin, to make us clean from all sin.

Therefore with Angels, etc.

### EPIPHANY

¶ *Upon the Epiphany, and seven days after.*

Through Jesus Christ our Lord; who, in substance of our mortal flesh, manifested forth his glory; that he might bring us out of darkness into his own glorious light.

Therefore with Angels, etc.

### PURIFICATION, ANNUNCIATION, AND TRANS-FIGURATION

¶ *Upon the Feasts of the Purification, Annunciation, and Transfiguration.*

Because in the Mystery of the Word made flesh, thou hast caused a new light to shine in our hearts, to give the knowledge of thy glory in the face of thy Son Jesus Christ our Lord.

Therefore with Angels, etc.

## EASTER

¶ *Upon Easter Day, and seven days after.*

But chiefly are we bound to praise thee for the glorious Resurrection of thy Son Jesus Christ our Lord: for he is the very Paschal Lamb, which was offered for us, and hath taken away the sin of the world; who by his death hath destroyed death, and by his rising to life again hath restored to us everlasting life.

Therefore with Angels, etc.

## ASCENSION

¶ *Upon Ascension Day, and seven days after.*

Through thy most dearly beloved Son Jesus Christ our Lord; who, after his most glorious Resurrection, manifestly appeared to all his Apostles, and in their sight ascended up into heaven, to prepare a place for us; that where he is, thither we might also ascend, and reign with him in glory.

Therefore with Angels, etc.

## WHITSUNTIDE

¶ *Upon Whitsunday, and six days after.*

Through Jesus Christ our Lord; according to whose most true promise, the Holy Ghost came down as at this time from heaven, lighting upon the disciples, to teach them, and to lead them into all truth; giving them boldness with fervent zeal constantly to preach the Gospel unto all nations; whereby we have been brought out of darkness and error into the clear light and true knowledge of thee, and of thy Son Jesus Christ.

Therefore with Angels, etc.

## TRINITY SUNDAY

¶ *Upon the Feast of Trinity only.*

Who, with thine only-begotten Son, and the Holy Ghost, art one God, one Lord, in Trinity of Persons and in Unity of Substance. For that which we believe of thy glory, O Father, the same we believe of the Son, and of the Holy Ghost, without any difference of inequality.

Therefore with Angels, etc.

¶ *Or this.*

For the precious death and merits of thy Son Jesus Christ our Lord, and for the sending to us of the Holy Ghost, the Comforter; who are one with thee in thy Eternal Godhead.

Therefore with Angels, etc.

## ALL SAINTS

¶ *Upon All Saints' Day, and seven days after.*

Who, in the multitude of thy Saints, hast compassed us about with so great a cloud of witnesses that we, rejoicing in their fellowship, may run with patience the race that is set before us, and, together with them, may receive the crown of glory that fadeth not away.

Therefore with Angels and Archangels, and with all the company of heaven, we laud and magnify thy glorious Name; evermore praising thee, and saying,

HOLY, HOLY, HOLY, Lord        God of hosts, Heaven and earth   ¶ *Priest and People.* are full of thy glory: Glory be to thee, O Lord Most High. Amen.

¶ *When the Priest, standing before the Holy Table, hath so ordered the Bread and Wine, that he may with the more readiness and decency break the Bread before the People, and take the Cup into his hands, he shall say the Prayer of Consecration, as followeth.*

All glory be to thee, Almighty God, our heavenly Father, for that thou, of thy tender mercy, didst give thine only Son Jesus Christ to suffer death upon the Cross for our redemption; who made there (by his one oblation of himself once offered) a full, perfect, and sufficient sacrifice, oblation, and satisfaction, for the sins of the whole world; and did institute, and in his holy Gospel command us to continue, a perpetual memory of that his precious death and sacrifice, until his coming again: For in the night in which he was betrayed, (*a*) he took Bread; and when he had given thanks, (*b*) he brake it, and gave it to his disciples, saying, Take, eat, (*c*) this is my Body, which is given for you; Do this in remembrance of me. Likewise, after supper, (*d*) he took the Cup; and when he had given thanks, he gave it to them, saying, Drink ye all of this; for (*e*) this is my Blood of the New Testament, which is shed for you, and for many, for the remission of sins; Do this, as oft as ye shall drink it, in remembrance of me.

*(a) Here the Priest is to take the Paten into his hands.*

*(b) And here to break the Bread.*

*(c) And here to lay his hand upon all the Bread.*

*(d) Here he is to take the Cup into his hands.*

*(e) And here he is to lay his hand upon every vessel in which there is any Wine to be consecrated.*

Wherefore, O Lord and heavenly Father, according to the institution of thy dearly beloved Son our Saviour Jesus Christ, we, thy humble servants, do celebrate and make here before thy Divine Majesty, with these thy holy gifts, which we now offer unto thee, the memorial thy Son hath commanded us to make: having in remembrance

*The Oblation.*

his blessed passion and precious death, his mighty resurrection and glorious ascension; rendering unto thee most hearty thanks for the innumerable benefits procured unto us by the same.

And we most humbly beseech thee, O merciful Father, to hear us; and, of *The Invocation.* thy almighty goodness, vouchsafe to bless and sanctify, with thy Word and Holy Spirit, these thy gifts and creatures of bread and wine; that we, receiving them according to thy Son our Saviour Jesus Christ's holy institution, in remembrance of his death and passion, may be partakers of his most blessed Body and Blood.

And we earnestly desire thy fatherly goodness, mercifully to accept this our sacrifice of praise and thanksgiving; most humbly beseeching thee to grant that, by the merits and death of thy Son Jesus Christ, and through faith in his blood, we, and all thy whole Church, may obtain remission of our sins, and all other benefits of his passion. And here we offer and present unto thee, O Lord, our selves, our souls and bodies, to be a reasonable, holy, and living sacrifice unto thee; humbly beseeching thee, that we, and all others who shall be partakers of this Holy Communion, may worthily receive the most precious Body and Blood of thy Son Jesus Christ, be filled with thy grace and heavenly benediction, and made one body with him, that he may dwell in us, and we in him. And although we are unworthy, through our manifold sins, to offer unto thee any sacrifice; yet we beseech thee to accept this our bounden duty and service; not weighing our merits, but pardoning our offences, through Jesus Christ our Lord; by whom, and with whom, in the unity of the Holy Ghost, all honour and glory be unto thee, O Father Almighty, world without end. *Amen.*

And now, as our Saviour Christ hath taught us, we are bold to say,

Our Father, who art in heaven, Hallowed be thy Name. Thy kingdom come. Thy will be done, On earth as it is in heaven. Give us this day our daily bread. And forgive us our trespasses, As we forgive those who trespass against us. And lead us not into temptation, But deliver us from evil. For thine is the kingdom, and the power, and the glory, for ever and ever. Amen.

¶ *Then shall the Priest, kneeling down at the Lord's Table, say, in the name of all those who shall receive the Communion, this Prayer following.*

We do not presume to come to this thy Table, O merciful Lord, trusting in our own righteousness, but in thy manifold and great mercies. We are not worthy so much as to gather up the crumbs under thy Table. But thou art the same Lord, whose property is always to have mercy: Grant us therefore, gracious Lord, so to eat the flesh of thy dear Son Jesus Christ, and to drink his blood, that our sinful bodies may be made clean by his body, and our souls washed through his most precious blood, and that we may evermore dwell in him, and he in us. *Amen.*

¶ *Here may be sung a Hymn.*

¶ *Then shall the Priest first receive the Holy Communion in both kinds himself, and proceed to deliver the same to the Bishops, Priests, and Deacons, in like manner, (if any be present) and, after that, to the People also in order, into their hands, all devoutly kneeling. And sufficient opportunity shall be given to those present to communicate. And when he delivereth the Bread, he shall say,*

The Body of our Lord Jesus Christ, which was given for thee, preserve thy body and soul unto everlasting life. Take and eat this in remembrance that Christ died for thee, and feed on him in thy heart by faith, with thanksgiving.

¶ *And the Minister who delivereth the Cup shall say,*

The Blood of our Lord Jesus Christ, which was shed for thee, preserve thy body and soul unto everlasting life. Drink this in remembrance that Christ's Blood was shed for thee, and be thankful.

¶ *If the consecrated Bread or Wine be spent before all have communicated, the Priest is to consecrate more, according to the Form before prescribed; beginning at,* All glory be to thee, Almighty God, *and ending with these words,* partakers of his most blessed Body and Blood.

¶ *When all have communicated, the Priest shall return to the Lord's Table, and reverently place upon it what remaineth of the consecrated Elements, covering the same with a fair linen cloth.*

¶ *Then shall the Priest say,*

### Let us pray.

Almighty and everliving God, we most heartily thank thee, for that thou dost vouchsafe to feed us who have duly received these holy mysteries, with the spiritual food of the most precious Body and Blood of thy Son our Saviour Jesus Christ; and dost assure us thereby of thy favour and goodness towards us; and that we are very members incorporate in the mystical body of thy Son, which is the blessed company of all faithful people; and are also heirs through hope of thy everlasting kingdom, by the merits of his most precious death and passion. And we humbly beseech thee, O heavenly Father, so to assist us with thy grace, that we may continue in that holy fellowship, and do all such good works as thou hast prepared for us to walk in; through Jesus Christ our Lord, to whom, with thee and the Holy Ghost, be all honour and glory, world without end. *Amen.*

# Holy Communion

¶ *Then shall be said the Gloria in excelsis, all standing, or some proper Hymn.*

Glory be to God on high, and on earth peace, good will towards men. We praise thee, we bless thee, we worship thee, we glorify thee, we give thanks to thee for thy great glory, O Lord God, heavenly King, God the Father Almighty.

O Lord, the only-begotten Son, Jesus Christ; O Lord God, Lamb of God, Son of the Father, that takest away the sins of the world, have mercy upon us. Thou that takest away the sins of the world, receive our prayer. Thou that sittest at the right hand of God the Father, have mercy upon us.

For thou only art holy; thou only art the Lord; thou only, O Christ, with the Holy Ghost, art most high in the glory of God the Father. Amen.

¶ *Then, the People kneeling, the Priest (the Bishop if he be present) shall let them depart with this Blessing.*

The Peace of God, which passeth all understanding, keep your hearts and minds in the knowledge and love of God, and of his Son Jesus Christ our Lord: And the Blessing of God Almighty, the Father, the Son, and the Holy Ghost, be amongst you, and remain with you always. *Amen.*


## GENERAL RUBRICS

¶ *In the absence of a Priest, a Deacon may say all that is before appointed unto the end of the Gospel.*

¶ *Upon the Sundays and other Holy Days, (though there be no Sermon or Communion,) may be said all that is appointed at the Communion, unto the end of the Gospel, concluding with the Blessing.*

¶ *And if any of the consecrated Bread and Wine remain after the Communion, it shall not be carried out of the Church; but the Minister and other Communicants shall, immediately after the Blessing, reverently eat and drink the same.*

¶ *If among those who come to be partakers of the Holy Communion, the Minister shall know any to be an open and notorious evil liver, or to have done any wrong to his neighbours by word or deed, so that the Congregation be thereby offended; he shall advertise him, that he presume not to come to the Lord's Table, until he have openly declared himself to have truly repented and amended his former evil life, that the Congregation may thereby be satisfied; and that he hath recompensed the parties to whom he hath done wrong; or at least declare himself to be in full purpose so to do, as soon as he conveniently may.*

¶ *The same order shall the Minister use with those, betwixt whom he perceiveth malice and hatred to reign; not suffering them to be partakers of the Lord's Table, until he know them to be reconciled. And if one of the parties, so at variance, be content to forgive from the bottom of his heart all that the other hath trespassed against him, and to make amends for that wherein he himself hath offended; and the other party will not be persuaded to a godly unity, but remain still in his frowardness and malice; the Minister in that case ought to admit the penitent person to the Holy Communion, and not him that is obstinate. Provided, That every Minister so repelling any, as is herein specified, shall be obliged to give an account of the same to the Ordinary, within fourteen days after, at the farthest.*

# TABLE OF EPISTLES AND GOSPELS
# FOR THE CHURCH YEAR

| SUNDAYS AND FESTIVALS | EPISTLE | GOSPEL |
|---|---|---|
| **ADVENT SEASON** | | |
| *1st Sunday in Advent* | Romans 13:8–14 | St. Matthew 21:1–13 |
| *2nd Sunday in Advent* | Romans 15:4–13 | St. Luke 21:25–33 |
| *3rd Sunday in Advent* | I Corinthians 4:1–5 | St. Matthew 11:2–10 |
| *4th Sunday in Advent* | Philippians 4:4–7 | St. John 1:19–28 |
| **CHRISTMAS DAY** | | |
| *(Dec. 25)* | Hebrews 1:1–13 | St. John 1:1–14 |
| | Titus 2:11–15 | St. Luke 2:1–14 |
| **ST. STEPHEN** *(Dec. 26)* | Acts 7:55–60 | St. Matthew 23:34–39 |
| **ST. JOHN** *(Dec. 27)* | I St. John 1:1–10 | St. John 21:19–25 |
| **THE HOLY INNO—** | | |
| **CENTS** *(Dec. 28)* | Revelation 14:1–5 | St. Matthew 2:13–18 |
| *1st Sunday after Christmas Day* | Galatians 4:1–7 | St. Matthew 1:18–25 |
| **THE CIRCUMCISION OF CHRIST** *(Jan. 1)* | Philippians 2:9–13 | St. Luke 2:15–21 |
| *2nd Sunday after Christmas Day* | Isaiah 61:1–3 | St. Matthew 2:19–23 |
| **THE EPIPHANY SEASON** | | |
| *The Epiphany (Jan. 6)* | Ephesians 3:1–12 | St. Matthew 2:1–12 |
| *1st Sunday after Epiphany* | Romans 12:1–5 | St. Luke 2:41–52 |
| *2nd Sunday after Epiphany* | Romans 12:6–16 | St. Mark 1:1–11 |
| *3rd Sunday after Epiphany* | Romans 12:16–21 | St. John 2:1–11 |
| *4th Sunday after Epiphany* | Romans 13:1–7 | St. Matthew 8:1–13 |
| *5th Sunday after Epiphany* | Colossians 3:12–17 | St. Matthew 13:24–30 |
| *6th Sunday after Epiphany* | I St. John 3:1–8 | St. Matthew 24:23–31 |
| **PRE-LENTEN SEASON** | | |
| *Septuagesima Sunday* | I Corinthians 9:24–27 | St. Matthew 20:1–16 |
| *Sexagesima Sunday* | 2 Corinthians 11:19–31 | St. Luke 8:4–15 |
| *Quinquagesima* | I Corinthians 13:1–13 | St. Luke 18:31–43 |

23

| Sundays and Festivals | Epistle | Gospel |
|---|---|---|
| *LENTEN SEASON* | | |
| *Ash Wednesday* | Joel 2:12–17 | St. Matthew 6:16–21 |
| *1st Sunday in Lent* | 2 Corinthians 6:1–10 | St. Matthew 4:1–11 |
| *2nd Sunday in Lent* | I Thessalonians 4:1–8 | St. Matthew 15:21–28 |
| *3rd Sunday in Lent* | Ephesians 5:1–14 | St. Luke 11:14–28 |
| *4th Sunday in Lent* | Galatians 4:21–31 | St. John 6:1–14 |
| *5th Sunday in Lent (Passion Sunday)* | Hebrews 9:11–15 | St. John 8:46–59 |
| *6th Sunday in Lent (Palm Sunday)* | Philippians 2:5–11 | St. Matthew 27:1–54 |
| *Monday before Easter* | Isaiah 63:1–19 | St. Mark 14:1–72 |
| *Tuesday before Easter* | Isaiah 50:5–11 | St. Mark 15:1–39 |
| *Wednesday before Easter* | Hebrews 9:16–28 | St. Luke 22:1–71 |
| *Thursday before Easter (Maundy)* | I Corinthians 11:23–26 | St. Luke 23:1–49 |
| | | St. John 13:1–15 |
| *Good Friday* | Hebrews 10:1–25 | St. John 19:1–37 |
| *Easter Even* | I St. Peter 3:17–22 | St. Matthew 27:57–66 |
| *EASTER DAY* | Colossians 3:1–4 | St. John 20:1–10 |
| | I Corinthians 5:6–8 | St. Mark 16:1–8 |
| *Monday in Easter Week* | Acts 10:34–43 | St. Luke 24:13–35 |
| *Tuesday in Easter Week* | Acts 13:26–41 | St. Luke 24:36–48 |
| *1st Sunday after Easter* | I St. John 5:4–12 | St. John 20:19–23 |
| *2nd Sunday after Easter* | I St. Peter 2:19–25 | St. John 10:11–16 |
| *3rd Sunday after Easter* | I St. Peter 2:11–17 | St. John 16:16–22 |
| *4th Sunday after Easter* | St. James 1:17–21 | St. John 16:5–15 |
| *5th Sunday after Easter (Rogation Sunday)* | St. James 1:22–27 | St. John 16:23–33 |
| *ASCENSIONTIDE* | | |
| *Ascension Day* | Acts I:1–11 | St. Luke 24:49–53 |
| *Sunday after Ascension Day* | I St. Peter 4:7–11 | St. John 15:26–27, 16:1–4 |
| *WHITSUNTIDE* | | |
| *Whitsunday (Pentecost)* | Acts 2:1–11 | St. John 14:15–31 |
| | I Corinthians 12:4–14 | St. Luke 11:9–13 |
| *Monday in Whitsun Week* | Acts 10:34–48 | St. John 3:16–21 |
| *Tuesday in Whitsun Week* | Acts 8:14–17 | St. John 10:1–10 |

| SUNDAYS AND FESTIVALS | EPISTLE | GOSPEL |
|---|---|---|
| **TRINITY SEASON** | | |
| Trinity Sunday | Revelation 4:1–11 | St. John 3:1–15 |
| 1st Sunday after Trinity | I St. John 4:7–21 | St. Luke 16:19–31 |
| 2nd Sunday after Trinity | I St. John 3:13–24 | St. Luke 14:16–24 |
| 3rd Sunday after Trinity | I St. Peter 5:5–11 | St. Luke 15:1–10 |
| 4th Sunday after Trinity | Romans 8:18–23 | St. Luke 6:36–42 |
| 5th Sunday after Trinity | I St. Peter 3:8–15 | St. Luke 5:1–11 |
| 6th Sunday after Trinity | Romans 6:3–11 | St. Matthew 5:20–26 |
| 7th Sunday after Trinity | Romans 6:19–23 | St. Mark 8:1–9 |
| 8th Sunday after Trinity | Romans 8:12–17 | St. Matthew 17:15–21 |
| 9th Sunday after Trinity | I Corinthians 10:1–13 | St. Luke 15:11–32 |
| 10th Sunday after Trinity | I Corinthians 12:1–11 | St. Luke 19:41–47 |
| 11th Sunday after Trinity | I Corinthians 15:1–11 | St. Luke 18:9–14 |
| 12th Sunday after Trinity | 2 Corinthians 3:4–9 | St. Mark 7:31–37 |
| 13th Sunday after Trinity | Galatians 3:16–22 | St. Luke 10:23–37 |
| 14th Sunday after Trinity | Galatians 5:16–24 | St. Luke 17:11–19 |
| 15th Sunday after Trinity | Galatians 6:11–18 | St. Matthew 6:24–34 |
| 16th Sunday after Trinity | Ephesians 3:13–21 | St. Luke 7:11–17 |
| 17th Sunday after Trinity | Ephesians 4:1–6 | St. Luke 14:1–11 |
| 18th Sunday after Trinity | I Corinthians 1:4–8 | St. Matthew 22:34–46 |
| 19th Sunday after Trinity | Ephesians 4:17–32 | St. Matthew 9:1–8 |
| 20th Sunday after Trinity | Ephesians 5:15–21 | St. Matthew 22:1–14 |
| 21st Sunday after Trinity | Ephesians 6:10–20 | St. John 4:46–54 |
| 22nd Sunday after Trinity | Philippians 1:3–11 | St. Matthew 18:21–35 |
| 23rd Sunday after Trinity | Philippians 3:17–21 | St. Matthew 22:15–22 |
| 24th Sunday after Trinity | Colossians 1:3–12 | St. Matthew 9:18–26 |
| The Sunday Next before Advent | Jeremiah 23:5–8 | St. John 6:5–14 |
| **HOLY DAYS** | | |
| St. Andrew the Apostle (Nov. 30) | Romans 10:9–21 | St. Matthew 4:18–22 |
| St. Thomas the Apostle (Dec. 21) | Hebrews 10:35–11:1 | St. John 20:24–31 |
| The Conversion of St. Paul (Jan. 25) | Acts 9:1–22 | St. Matthew 19:27–30 |
| The Presentation of Christ in the Temple (Feb. 2) | Malachi 3:1–5 | St. Luke 2:22–40 |
| St. Matthias the Apostle (Feb. 24) | Acts 1:15–26 | St. Matthew 11:25–30 |

| SUNDAYS AND FESTIVALS | EPISTLE | GOSPEL |
|---|---|---|
| *The Annunciation of The Blessed Virgin Mary (Mar. 25)* | Isaiah 7:10–15 | St. Luke 1:26–38 |
| *St. Mark the Evangelist (Apr. 25)* | Ephesians 4:7–16 | St. John 15:1–11 |
| *St. Philip and St. James, Apostles (May 1)* | St. James 1:1–12 | St. John 14:1–14 |
| *St. Barnabas the Apostle (June 11)* | Acts 11:22–30 | St. John 15:12–16 |
| *St. John Baptist (June 24)* | Isaiah 40:1–11 | St. Luke 1:57–80 |
| *St. Peter the Apostle (June 29)* | Acts 12:1–11 | St. Matthew 16:13–1 |
| *St. James the Apostle (July 25)* | Acts 11:27–12:3 | St. Matthew 20:20–2 |
| *The Transfiguration of Christ (Aug. 6)* | St. Peter 1:13–18 | St. Luke 9:28–36 |
| *St. Bartholomew the Apostle (Aug. 24)* | Acts 5:12–16 | St. Luke 22:24–30 |
| *St. Matthew, Apostle and Evangelist (Sept. 21)* | 2 Corinthians 4:1–6 | St. Matthew 9:9–13 |
| *St. Michael and All Angels (Sept. 29)* | Revelation 12:7–12 | St. Matthew 18:1–10 |
| *St. Luke the Evangelist (Oct. 18)* | 2 Timothy 4:5–15 | St. Luke 10:1–7 |
| *St. Simon and St. Jude, Apostles (Oct. 28)* | Ephesians 2:19–22 | St. John 15:17–27 |
| *All Saints' Day (Nov. 1)* | Revelation 7:2–17 | St. Matthew 5:1–12 |
| *A Saint's Day* | Hebrews 12:1–2 | St. Matthew 25:31–4 |
| *Feast of the Dedication of a Church* | I St. Peter 2:1–5 | St. Matthew 21:12–1 |
| *The Ember Days (At the Four Seasons)* | Acts 13:44–49 | St. Luke 4:16–21 |
| *The Rogation Days* | Ezekiel 34:25–31 | St. Luke 11:5–13 |
| *Independence Day (July 4)* | Deuteronomy 10:17–21 | St. Matthew 5:43–48 |
| *Thanksgiving Day* | St. James 1:16–27 | St. Matthew 6:25–3 |
| *At a Marriage* | Ephesians 5:20–33 | St. Matthew 19:4–6 |
| *At the Burial of the Dead* | I Thessalonians 6:13–18 | St. John 6:37–40 |

# Spiritual Communion

¶ *If on any Sunday or other Day of Obligation (see Tables and Rules for the Movable and Immovable Feasts in the front part of the Prayer Book), you are prevented from making your Communion, make an act of Spiritual Communion, after the following manner:*

¶ *Kneel down, and say:*

In the name of the Father, and of the Son, and of the Holy Ghost, Amen.

¶ *Then read the Collect for the day, the Epistle, and the Holy Gospel.*

¶ *Rise and say the Nicene Creed.*

I believe in one God the Father Almighty, Maker of heaven and earth, And of all things visible and invisible:

And in one Lord Jesus Christ, the only-begotten Son of God; Begotten of His Father before all worlds, God of God, Light of Light, Very God of very God; Begotten, not made; Being of one substance with the Father; By whom all things were made: Who for us men and for our salvation came down from heaven, and was incarnate by the Holy Ghost of the Virgin Mary, and was made man: And was crucified also for us under Pontius Pilate; He suffered and was buried: And the third day He rose again according to the Scriptures: And ascended into heaven, And sitteth on the right hand of the Father: And he shall come again, with glory, to judge both the quick and the dead; Whose kingdom shall have no end.

And I believe in the Holy Ghost, The Lord, and Giver of Life, Who proceedeth from the Father and the Son; Who with the Father and the Son together is worshipped and glorified; Who spake by the Prophets: And I believe one Catholic and Apostolic Church:

I acknowledge one Baptism for the remission of sins:
And I look for the Resurrection of the dead: And the
Life of the world to come. Amen.

*¶ Kneel and read the Confession*

Almighty God, Father of our Lord Jesus Christ,
Maker of all things, Judge of all men; We acknowledge
and bewail our manifold sins and wickedness, Which
we, from time to time, most grievously have committed, By thought, word, and deed, Against Thy
Divine Majesty, Provoking most justly Thy wrath
and indignation against us. We do earnestly repent,
And are heartily sorry for these our misdoings: The
remembrance of them is grievous unto us; The burden
of them is intolerable. Have mercy upon us, Have
mercy upon us, most merciful Father; For Thy Son
our Lord Jesus Christ's sake, Forgive us all that is
past; And grant that we may ever hereafter Serve
and please Thee In newness of life, To the honour and
glory of Thy Name; Through Jesus Christ our Lord.
Amen.

*¶ Then say:*

The Almighty and merciful Lord, grant me pardon
and absolution of all my sins. Amen.

*¶ Read the Comfortable Words, Preface, and Sanctus.*

Hear what comfortable words our Saviour Christ
saith unto all who truly turn to Him.

Come unto Me, all ye that travail and are heavy
laden, and I will refresh you. *St. Matt.* xi. 28.

So God loved the world, that He gave His only-
begotten Son, to the end that all that believe in Him
should not perish, but have everlasting life. *St. John*
iii. 16.

Hear also what Saint Paul saith.

This is a true saying, and worthy of all men to be received, That Christ Jesus came into the world to save sinners. *I Tim.* i. 15.

Hear also what Saint John saith.

If any man sin, we have an Advocate with the Father, Jesus Christ the Righteous; and He is the Propitiation for our sins. *I St. John* ii. 1, 2.

Therefore with Angels and Archangels, and with all the company of heaven, we laud and magnify Thy glorious Name; evermore praising Thee, and saying,

HOLY, HOLY, HOLY, Lord God of hosts, Heaven and earth are full of Thy glory: Glory be to Thee, O Lord Most High. Amen.

*¶ Then say:*

In union, O Lord, with the faithful at every altar of Thy Church, where the Holy Eucharist is now being celebrated, I desire to offer Thee praise and thanksgiving. I present to Thee my soul and body with the earnest wish that I may always be united to Thee, And since I can not now receive Thee sacramentally, I beseech Thee to come spiritually into my heart. I unite myself to Thee, and embrace Thee with all the affections of my soul. Let nothing ever separate Thee from me. May I live and die in Thy love. Amen.

*¶ Spend a few moments in meditation upon the fact that God so loved you that He sent His Only-Begotten Son into the world for you. Recite the Lord's Prayer and afterward say:*

May the grace of our Lord Jesus Christ, and the love of God, and the fellowship of the Holy Ghost, be with me always. Amen.

# The Ministration of
# Holy Baptism

¶ *The Minister of every Parish shall often admonish the People, that they defer not the Baptism of their Children, and that it is most convenient that Baptism should be administered upon Sundays and other Holy Days. Nevertheless, if necessity so require, Baptism may be administered upon any other day. And also he shall warn them that, except for urgent cause, they seek not to have their Children baptized in their houses.*

¶ *There shall be for every Male-child to be baptized, when they can be had, two Godfathers and one Godmother; and for every Female, one Godfather and two Godmothers; and Parents shall be admitted as Sponsors if it be desired.*

¶ *When there are Children to be baptized, the Parents or Sponsors shall give knowledge thereof to their Minister. And then the Godfathers and Godmothers, and the People with the Children, must be ready at the Font, either immediately after the Second Lesson at Morning or Evening Prayer, or at such other time as the Minister shall appoint.*

¶ *When any such Persons as are of riper years are to be baptized, timely notice shall be given to the Minister; that so due care may be taken for their examination, whether they be sufficiently instructed in the Principles of the Christian Religion; and that they may be exhorted to prepare themselves, with Prayers and Fasting, for the receiving of this holy Sacrament.*

¶ *And* NOTE, *that at the time of the Baptism of an Adult, there shall be present with him at the Font at least two Witnesses.*

¶ *The Minister, having come to the Font, which is then to be filled with pure Water, shall say as followeth, the People all standing,*

Hath this Child (Person) been already baptized, or no?

¶ *If they answer,* No: *then shall the Minister proceed as followeth.*

Dearly beloved, forasmuch as our Saviour Christ saith, None can enter into the kingdom of God, except he be regenerated and born anew of Water and of the

31

Holy Ghost; I beseech you to call upon God the Father, through our Lord Jesus Christ, that of his bounteous mercy he will grant to *this Child* (*this Person*) that which by nature *he* cannot have; that *he* may be baptized with Water and the Holy Ghost, and received into Christ's holy Church, and be made a living *member* of the same.

¶ *Then shall the Minister say,*

Let us pray.

Almighty and immortal God, the aid of all who need, the helper of all who flee to thee for succour, the life of those who believe, and the resurrection of the dead; We call upon thee for *this Child* (*this thy Servant*), that *he*, coming to thy holy Baptism, may receive remission of sin, by spiritual regeneration. Receive *him*, O Lord, as thou hast promised by thy well-beloved Son, saying, Ask, and ye shall have; seek, and ye shall find; knock, and it shall be opened unto you. So give now unto us who ask; let us who seek, find; open the gate unto us who knock; that *this Child* (*this thy Servant*) may enjoy the everlasting benediction of thy heavenly washing, and may come to the eternal kingdom which thou hast promised by Christ our Lord. *Amen.*

¶ *Then the Minister shall say as followeth.*

Hear the words of the Gospel, written by Saint Mark, in the tenth Chapter, at the thirteenth Verse.

They brought young children to Christ, that he should touch them: and his disciples rebuked those that brought them. But when Jesus saw it, he was much displeased, and said unto them, Suffer the little children to come unto me, and forbid them not: for of such is the kingdom of God. Verily I say unto you, Whosoever shall not receive the kingdom of God as a little child, he shall not enter therein. And he took them up in his arms, put his hands upon them, and blessed them.

¶ *Or this.*

Hear the words of the Gospel, written by Saint John, in the third Chapter, at the first Verse.

There was a man of the Pharisees, named Nicodemus, a ruler of the Jews: the same came to Jesus by night, and said unto him, Rabbi, we know that thou art a teacher come from God: for no man can do these miracles that thou doest, except God be with him. Jesus answered and said unto him, Verily, verily, I say unto thee, Except a man be born again, he cannot see the kingdom of God. Nicodemus saith unto him, How can a man be born when he is old? can he enter the second time into his mother's womb, and be born? Jesus answered, Verily, verily, I say unto thee, Except a man be born of water and of the Spirit, he cannot enter the kingdom of God. That which is born of flesh is flesh; and that which is born of the Spirit is spirit. Marvel not that I said unto thee, Ye must be born again. The wind bloweth where it listeth, and thou hearest the sound thereof, but canst not tell whence it cometh, and whither it goeth; so is every one that is born of the Spirit.

¶ *Or this.*

Hear the words of the Gospel, written by Saint Matthew, in the twenty-eighth Chapter, at the eighteenth Verse.

Jesus came and spake unto them, saying, All power is given unto me in heaven and in earth. Go ye therefore, and make disciples of all nations, baptizing them in the name of the Father, and of the Son, and of the Holy Ghost: teaching them to observe all things whatsoever I have commanded you: and, lo, I am with you alway, even unto the end of the world.

¶ *Then shall the Minister say,*

And now, being persuaded of the good will of our heavenly Father toward *this Child (this Person),* declared by his Son Jesus Christ; let us faithfully and devoutly give thanks unto him, and say,

Almighty and everlasting God, heavenly Father, We give these humble thanks, That thou hast vouchsafed to call us To the knowledge of thy grace, and faith in thee: Increase this knowledge, And confirm this faith in us evermore. Give thy Holy Spirit to *this Child (this thy Servant),* That *he* may be born again, And be made *an heir* of everlasting salvation; Through our Lord Jesus Christ, Who liveth and reigneth with thee and the same Holy Spirit, Now and for ever. Amen. ¶ *Minister and People,*

¶ *When the Office is used for Children, the Minister shall speak unto the Godfathers and Godmothers on this wise.*

Dearly beloved, ye have brought *this Child* here to be baptized; ye have prayed that our Lord Jesus Christ would vouchsafe to receive *him,* to release *him* from sin, to sanctify *him* with the Holy Ghost, to give *him* the kingdom of heaven, and everlasting life.

Dost thou, therefore, in the name of this Child, renounce the devil and all his works, the vain pomp and glory of the world, with all covetous desires of the same, and the sinful desires of the flesh, so that thou wilt not follow, nor be led by them?

*Answer.* I renounce them all; and, by God's help, will endeavour not to follow, nor be led by them.

*Minister.* Dost thou believe all the Articles of the Christian Faith, as contained in the Apostles' Creed?

*Answer.* I do.

*Minister.* Wilt thou be baptized in this Faith?

*Answer.* That is my desire.

*Minister.* Wilt thou then obediently keep God's holy will and commandments, and walk in the same all the days of thy life?

*Answer.* I will, by God's help.

*Minister.* Having now, in the name of this Child, made these promises, wilt thou also on thy part take heed that this Child learn the Creed, the Lord's Prayer, and the Ten Commandments, and all other things which a Christian ought to know and believe to his soul's health?

*Answer.* I will, by God's help.

*Minister.* Wilt thou take heed that this Child, so soon as sufficiently instructed, be brought to the Bishop to be confirmed by him?

*Answer.* I will, God being my helper.

¶ *When the Office is used for Adults, the Minister shall address them on this wise, the Persons to be baptized answering the questions for themselves.*

Well-Beloved, you have come hither desiring to receive holy Baptism. We have prayed that our Lord Jesus Christ would vouchsafe to receive you, to release you from sin, to sanctify you with the Holy Ghost, to give you the kingdom of heaven, and everlasting life.

Dost thou renounce the devil and all his works, the vain pomp and glory of the world, with all covetous desires of the same, and the sinful desires of the flesh, so that thou wilt not follow, nor be led by them?

*Answer.* I renounce them all; and, by God's help, will endeavour not to follow, nor be led by them.

*Minister.* Dost thou believe in Jesus the Christ, the Son of the Living God?

*Answer.* I do.

*Minister.* Dost thou accept him, and desire to follow him as thy Saviour and Lord?

*Answer.* I do.

*Minister.* Dost thou believe all the Articles of the Christian Faith, as contained in the Apostles' Creed?

*Answer.* I do.

*Minister.* Wilt thou be baptized in this Faith?

*Answer.* That is my desire.

*Minister.* Wilt thou then obediently keep God's holy will and commandments, and walk in the same all the days of thy life?

*Answer.* I will, by God's help.

¶ *Then shall the Minister say,*

O Merciful God, grant that like as Christ died and rose again, so *this Child* (*this thy Servant*) may die to sin and rise to newness of life. *Amen.*

Grant that all sinful affections may die in *him*, and that all things belonging to the Spirit may live and grow in *him*. *Amen.*

Grant that *he* may have power and strength to have victory, and to triumph, against the devil, the world, and the flesh. *Amen.*

Grant that whosoever is here dedicated to thee by our office and ministry, may also be endued with heavenly virtues, and everlastingly rewarded, through thy mercy, O blessed Lord God, who dost live, and govern all things, world without end. *Amen.*

# Holy Baptism

*Minister.* The Lord be with you.

*Answer.* And with thy spirit.

*Minister.* Lift up your hearts.

*Answer.* We lift them up unto the Lord.

*Minister.* Let us give thanks unto our Lord God.

*Answer.* It is meet and right so to do.

¶ *Then the Minister shall say,*

It is very meet, right, and our bounden duty, that we should give thanks unto thee, O Lord, Holy Father, Almighty, Everlasting God, for that thy dearly beloved Son Jesus Christ, for the forgiveness of our sins, did shed out of his most precious side both water and blood; and gave commandment to his disciples, that they should go teach all nations, and baptize them In the Name of the Father, and of the Son, and of the Holy Ghost. Regard, we beseech thee, the supplications of thy congregation; sanctify this Water to the mystical washing away of sin; and grant that *this Child* (*this* thy *Servant*), now to be baptized therein, may receive the fulness of thy grace, and ever remain in the number of thy faithful children; through the same Jesus Christ our Lord, to whom, with thee, in the unity of the Holy Spirit, be all honour and glory, now and evermore. *Amen.*

¶ *Then the Minister shall take the Child into his arms, and shall say to the Godfathers and Godmothers,*

### Name this Child.

¶ *And then, naming the Child after them, he shall dip him in the Water discreetly, or shall pour water upon him, saying,*

N. I baptize thee In the Name of the Father, and of the Son, and of the Holy Ghost. Amen.

¶ *But* NOTE, *That if the Person to be baptized be an Adult, the Minister shall take him by the hand, and shall ask the Witnesses the Name; and then shall dip him in the Water, or pour Water upon him, using the same form of words.*

¶ *Then the Minister shall say,*

We Receive this Child (Person) into the congregation of Christ's flock; and do * sign *him* with the sign of the Cross in token that hereafter *he* shall not be ashamed to confess the faith of Christ crucified, and manfully to fight under his banner, against sin, the world, and the devil;

\* *Here the Minister shall make a Cross upon the Child's (or Person's) forehead.*

and to continue Christ's faithful soldier and servant unto *his* life's end. Amen.

¶ *Then shall the Minister say,*

Seeing now, dearly beloved brethren, that *this Child (this Person) is* regenerate, and grafted into the body of Christ's Church, let us give thanks unto Almighty God for these benefits; and with one accord make our prayers unto him, that *this Child (this Person)* may lead the rest of *his* life according to this beginning.

¶ *Then shall be said,*

Our Father, who art in heaven, Hallowed be thy Name. Thy kingdom come. Thy will be done, On earth as it is in heaven. Give us this day our daily bread. And forgive us our trespasses, As we forgive those who trespass against us. And lead us not into temptation, But deliver us from evil. For thine is the kingdom, and the power, and the glory, for ever and ever. Amen.

¶ *Then shall the Minister say,*

We yield thee hearty thanks, most merciful Father, that it hath pleased thee to regenerate *this Child (this* thy *Servant)* with thy Holy Spirit, to receive *him* for thine own *Child,* and to incorporate *him* into thy holy

Church. And humbly we beseech thee to grant, that *he*, being dead unto sin, may live unto righteousness, and being buried with Christ in his death, may also be *partaker* of his resurrection; *so* that finally, with the residue of thy holy Church, *he* may be *an inheritor* of thine everlasting kingdom; through Christ our Lord. *Amen.*

¶ *Then the Minister shall add,*

The Almighty God, the Father of our Lord Jesus Christ, of whom the whole family in heaven and earth is named; Grant you to be strengthened with might by his Spirit in the inner man; that, Christ dwelling in your hearts by faith, ye may be filled with all the fulness of God. *Amen.*

¶ *It is expedient that every Adult, thus baptized, should be confirmed by the Bishop, so soon after his Baptism as conveniently may be; that so he may be admitted to the Holy Communion.*

# Baptism in Extremis

If a dying comrade has not been baptized and wants to be; and no Chaplain is within reach; *you* can baptize your friend. Pour a little water on the brow (or any other place if brow is hurt or bandaged) 3 times, saying his first name, as "John" and this:

I baptize thee in the Name of the Father, and of the Son, and of the Holy Ghost. Amen.

Sign him with the sign of the cross and say the *Our Father* . . .

If your comrade expires, say this Commendation over him:

Depart, O Christian soul, out of this world,
In the Name of God the Father Almighty who created thee.
In the Name of Jesus Christ who redeemed thee.
In the Name of the Holy Ghost who sanctifies thee.
May thy rest be this day in peace, and thy dwelling-place in the Paradise of God.

(Give Chaplain the facts, when you can.)

# The Way of Penitence

"Confession is good for the soul." So runs the ancient proverb, the crystallized verdict of human experience.

Just as the first step in bodily healing is to relieve tension and discharge poisons, so the spirit of man must have relief by telling his troubles to someone. The final "Someone" is always God. But most of us find that a sympathetic human listener helps us to tell God.

Therefore the Church, while providing a confessional moment in all her regular services, also says through her priest:

"If there be any of you who by this (general) means cannot quiet his own conscience, but requireth further comfort or counsel, let him come to me, or to some other Minister of God's Word, and open his grief." (*From an exhortation after the Communion Office, Book of Common Prayer, page 88*).

The Church in ordaining her priests says in Christ's Name to them: "Whose sins thou dost forgive, they are forgiven."

Upon the next page we give for those who desire to use it the main part of a more formal and yet very intimate type of confession. Being private and strictly confidential, it is not in the Prayer Book, but has been used from ancient times. For the sick room, this form is shortened here.

*This form of confession requires privacy whether in a church, home, hospital, or other place. It is usually best to arrange with the clergy in advance for this serv-*

*ice, but any priest is ready and willing to hear a confession on the spur of the moment if there is emergency.*

*The Act always begins with a Blessing for which the penitent asks.*

*Chaplain.* The Lord be in thy heart and upon thy lips, that so thou mayest worthily confess all thy sins, in the Name of the Father, and of the Son, and of the Holy Ghost. Amen.

*Penitent.* I confess to God Almighty; the Father, the Son, and the Holy Ghost; that I have sinned very much in thought, word, and deed, by my own fault. And especially I remember these sins;............

*(There are several variants of the above. The penitent then states the specific sins he can remember, and should end with the following:)*

*Penitent.* For these and all my other sins, which I cannot now remember, I am very sorry, I promise to do better, I beg God to forgive me; and you, Chaplain, to give me penance, advice and absolution.

*After the uninterrupted confession, the chaplain may find it helpful to question the penitent, so that advice about possible reparation, or restitution, or how to face the future more successfully may be given.*

*Then some form of penance is given. This is not a penalty but some useful act which aids the penitent to make outward embodiment of his contrite purpose. Then the chaplain gives the Absolution in these words with the sign of the Cross:*

ABSOLUTION. ¶ *The assurance of God's forgiveness.*

*Chaplain.* Almighty God, our heavenly Father, who of his great mercy hath promised forgiveness of sins to all those who with hearty repentance and true faith turn unto him; Have mercy upon you; pardon and deliver you from all your sins; confirm and strengthen you in all goodness; and bring you to everlasting life; through Jesus Christ our Lord. Amen.

*Then, always, the Blessing:*

*Chaplain.* The blessing of God Almighty, the Father, the Son, and the Holy Ghost, be upon thee and remain with thee always. Amen.

Go (*or*, Abide) in peace; the Lord hath put away all thy sins.

# Prayers

## IN THE MORNING

Into thy hands, O God, I commend myself this day. Let thy presence be with me even to its close, that at night I may again give thanks unto thee; through Jesus Christ our Lord. *Amen.*

Grant, O Lord, that I may not be ashamed to confess the faith of Christ crucified, and manfully to fight under his banner against sin, the world, and the devil, and to continue Christ's faithful soldier and servant unto my life's end. *Amen.*

Defend, O Lord, this thy Child with thy heavenly grace; that I may continue thine for ever; and daily increase in thy Holy Spirit more and more, until I come unto thy everlasting kingdom. *Amen.*

## AT NIGHT

O Lord, support us all the day long, until the shadows lengthen and the evening comes, and the busy world is hushed, and the fever of life is over, and our work is done. Then in thy mercy grant us a safe lodging, and a holy rest, and peace at the last. *Amen.*

The God of peace himself sanctify me wholly, and may my spirit and soul and body be preserved entire without blame at the coming of our Lord Jesus Christ. *Amen.*

Abide with us, O Lord, this night, and with all the sick and sorrowful, the forsaken and weary, to strengthen and to cheer, and to give rest. *Amen.*

Thine is the day, O Lord, and thine the night;
Grant that the sun of righteousness may abide in our
hearts, to drive away the darkness of evil thoughts;
through Jesus Christ our Lord. *Amen.*

O Lord, Lover of men, who forgivest us our sins;
Cleanse us of all that is base or selfish, and make us
to be in all things thy servants, and the messengers
of thy love. *Amen.*

Grant, O Lord, that we may meet all difficulties
and temptations with a stedfast heart, in the strength
of thy indwelling spirit. *Amen.*

Shield us, O God, from the darkness of soul which
seeth thee not, and from the loneliness of heart which
heareth not thy voice, and through life and in the
valley of the shadow of death, forsake us not; for thy
Name's sake. *Amen.*

Deepen and quicken in us, O God, a sense of thy
Presence, and make us to know and feel that thou art
more ready to teach and to give than we to ask or to
learn; through Jesus Christ our Lord. *Amen.*

O most merciful Redeemer, Friend, and Brother,
May I know thee more clearly,
May I love thee more dearly,
May I follow thee more nearly. *Amen.*

O Saviour of the world, who by thy Cross and
precious Blood hast redeemed us; Save us, and help
us, we humbly beseech thee, O Lord. *Amen.*

### ON ENTERING CHURCH

O Lord, I am in thy holy House. Help me to keep
my thoughts on thee, that I may hear thee speaking
in my heart, through Jesus Christ. *Amen.*

## At Early Eucharist

As watchmen look for the morning, so do we look for thee, O Christ. Come with the dawning day, and make thyself known to us in the breaking of Bread, for thou art our God for ever and ever. *Amen.*

## Before Holy Communion

Incline our hearts, O God, that by the grace of thy Holy Spirit we may worthily approach these sacred mysteries and offer ourselves to thee in answering love, through Jesus Christ our Lord. *Amen.*

## After Church Service

Sanctify, O Lord, both our coming in and our going forth; and grant that when we leave thy House we may not leave thy Presence, but be thou ever near unto us and keep us near unto thee, through Jesus Christ our Lord. *Amen.*

## An Act of Adoration

Worthy art thou, O God, to receive the honour and the power; for thou didst create all things, and because of thy will they are and were created.

*Glory be to thee, O God.*

Glory to thee, O Christ, who didst redeem with thy love men of every kindred and tongue and people and nation.

*Glory be to thee, O Christ.*

Glory to thee, O Holy Spirit, for thy work in the Church, which will not cease until thou hast made of all mankind one family, to the praise and glory of God.

*Glory be to thee, O Holy Spirit.*

## FOR GOD'S HELP

Grant us, O Lord, in all our duties thy help, in all our perplexities thy counsel, in all our dangers thy protection, and in all our sorrows thy peace; for the sake of Jesus Christ our Saviour. *Amen.*

Grant to us, Lord, we beseech thee, the spirit to think and do always such things as are right; that we, who cannot do anything that is good without thee, may by thee be enabled to live according to thy will; through Jesus Christ our Lord. *Amen.*

## FOR GOD'S PROTECTION

O Almighty and most merciful God, of thy bountiful goodness keep us, we beseech thee, from all things that may hurt us; that we, being ready both in body and soul, may cheerfully accomplish those things which thou commandest; through Jesus Christ our Lord. *Amen.*

We beseech thee, Almighty God, look upon the hearty desires of thy humble servants, and stretch forth the right hand of thy Majesty, to be our defence against all our enemies; through Jesus Christ our Lord. *Amen.*

## FOR AID AGAINST PERILS

Lighten our darkness, we beseech thee, O Lord; and by thy great mercy defend us from all perils and dangers of this night; for the love of thy only Son, our Saviour, Jesus Christ. *Amen.*

## FOR GOD'S MERCY

O God, the protector of all that trust in thee, without whom nothing is strong, nothing is holy; Increase and multiply upon us thy mercy; that, thou being our ruler and guide, we may so pass through things temporal, that we finally lose not the things eternal. Grant this, O heavenly Father, for the sake of Jesus Christ our Lord. *Amen.*

## FOR GUIDANCE OF THE HOLY SPIRIT

O God, forasmuch as without thee we are not able to please thee; Mercifully grant that thy Holy Spirit may in all things direct and rule our hearts; through Jesus Christ our Lord. *Amen.*

## FOR CHRISTIAN GLADNESS

O God, Author of the world's joy, Bearer of the world's pain; At the heart of all our trouble and sorrow let unconquerable gladness dwell; through our Lord and Saviour Jesus Christ. *Amen.*

## FOR THE COMPANIONSHIP OF CHRIST

O blessed Christ, who didst draw near to thy disciples as they walked together by the way and were sad; So draw near to us as we journey along our daily way. Open to us the meaning of life, and reveal thyself as our strength and our companion; as thou art our Lord and Saviour evermore. *Amen.*

## FOR VICTORY OVER TEMPTATION

Grant us, O Lord, to pass this day in gladness and peace, without stumbling and without stain; that, reaching the eventide victorious over all temptation, we may praise thee, the eternal God, who art blessed, and dost govern all things, world without end. *Amen.*

### FOR CONTROL OF SPEECH

O God, who knowest how often we sin against thee with our tongues; keep us free from all untrue, unkind, irreverent or unclean words; consecrate our speech to thy service; and keep us often silent, that our hearts may speak to thee and may listen for thy voice; through Jesus Christ our Lord. *Amen.*

### FOR THOSE WE LOVE

Almighty God, we entrust all who are dear to us to thy never-failing care and love, for this life and the life to come; knowing that thou art doing for them better things than we can desire or pray for; through Jesus Christ our Lord. *Amen.*

### FOR LOYALTY TO OUR HOMES

Grant, O Lord, to those in the service of their country who have left wives and children at home, a stedfast loyalty through all the days of separation, that returning at length to their beloved they may know the joy of unbroken fidelity; through Jesus Christ our Lord. *Amen.*

### FOR FIDELITY

Teach us, good Lord, to serve thee as thou deservest; to give and not to count the cost; to fight and not to heed the wounds: to toil and not to seek for rest; to labour and not to ask for any reward, save that of knowing that we do thy will; through Jesus Christ our Lord. *Amen.*

### FOR LOYALTY

Almighty God, grant us thy gift of loyalty. For our homes, give us love and obedience; for our country, sacrifice and service; for our Church, reverence and devotion; and in everything make us true to thee; through thy Son, our Saviour Jesus Christ. *Amen.*

## For Courage

O Thou, who art heroic love: Keep alive in our hearts that adventurous spirit which makes men scorn the way of safety, so that thy will be done. For so only, O Lord, shall we be worthy of those courageous souls who in every age have ventured all in obedience to thy call; through Jesus Christ our Lord. *Amen.*

## For Stedfastness

O God, Who rulest the world from everlasting to everlasting: Speak to our hearts when courage fails, and we faint for fear; when our love grows cold, and there is distress of nations upon the earth. Keep us resolute and stedfast in the things that cannot be shaken, abounding in hope and knowing that our labor is not in vain in thee. Deepen our faith in thine eternal purpose; renew in us that love which never fails; and make us to lift up our eyes to behold, beyond the things which are seen and temporal, the things which are unseen and eternal. We ask all in the Name of Jesus Christ our Lord. *Amen.*

## For Grace to Forgive

Merciful God, in whose dear Son we have redemption, even the forgiveness of sins; give us such strong belief in this the only power that can abolish evil that we shall be enabled to forgive our enemies; and grant us grace not only to forgive but to accept forgiveness through Christ, the crucified. *Amen.*

### For a Day of Battle

Heavenly Father, on a day of battle I commit myself body and soul to thy keeping. When I am in peril of life give me courage to do my duty. When I am tempted to sin give me strength to resist. If I am sick or wounded grant me healing. If I fall, of thy mercy receive me to thyself, forgiving me all my sins. Bless all who are near and dear to me and keep them in thy fatherly care. And in thy good providence, out of this evil bring a lasting peace; through Jesus Christ our Lord. *Amen.*

### For the Nation

O eternal God, through whose mighty power our fathers won their liberties of old; Grant, we beseech thee, that we and all the people of this land may have grace to maintain these liberties in righteousness and peace; through Jesus Christ our Lord. *Amen.*

### For All in the Service of our Country

O Almighty Lord God, who neither slumberest nor sleepest; Protect and assist, we beseech thee, all those who at home or abroad, by land, by sea, or in the air, are serving this country, that they, being armed with thy defense, may be preserved evermore in all perils; and being filled with wisdom and girded with strength, may do their duty to thy honour and glory; through Jesus Christ our Lord. *Amen.*

### For our Armed Forces

Heavenly Father, we commend to thy gracious care and keeping all the men and women in our Armed Forces at home and abroad. Defend them day by day with thy heavenly grace; strengthen them in their trials and temptations; give them courage to face the perils that beset them; and help them to know that none can pluck out of thy hand those who put their trust in thee; through Jesus Christ our Lord. *Amen.*

O Eternal God, we commend to thy fatherly care all those who are enlisted in the Armed Forces. In time of preparation grant that discipline and training may fit them worthily to serve our country, and in the day of strife guide and sustain them in upholding the cause of justice and freedom; through Jesus Christ our Lord. *Amen.*

## FOR SERVICEMEN AND SERVICEWOMEN

Almighty Father, we commit to thy loving care all those servicemen and servicewomen upon whose faithfulness the welfare of our Armed Forces depends. In the fulfilment of their duties give them patience, loyalty, and courage; and grant that those who are sustained by their toil may remember them with gratitude; through Jesus Christ our Lord. *Amen.*

## FOR THE ARMY

O Lord God of Hosts, stretch forth, we pray thee, thine almighty arm to strengthen and protect the soldiers of our country. Support them in the day of battle, and in the times of rest and training keep them safe from all evil; endue them with courage and loyalty; and grant that in all things they may serve without reproach; through Jesus Christ our Lord. *Amen.*

## FOR THE NAVY

O eternal Lord God, who alone spreadest out the heavens, and rulest the raging of the sea; Vouchsafe to take into thy almighty and most gracious protection our country's Navy, and all who serve therein. Preserve them from the dangers of the sea, and from the violence of the enemy; that they may be a safeguard unto the United States of America, and a security for such as pass on the seas upon their lawful occasions; that the inhabitants of our land may in peace and quietness serve thee our God, to the glory of thy Name; through Jesus Christ our Lord. *Amen.*

## FOR THE AIR FORCE

O Lord God of hosts, who stretchest out the heavens like a curtain; Watch over and protect, we pray thee, the airmen of our country as they fly upon their appointed tasks. Give them courage as they face the foe, and skill in the performance of their duty. Sustain them with thy Everlasting Arms. May thy hand lead them and thy right hand hold them up that they may return to the earth with a grateful sense of thy mercy; through Jesus Christ our Lord. *Amen.*

## FOR THE MARINE CORPS

O Eternal Father, we commend to thy protection and care the members of the Marine Corps. Guide and direct them in the defense of our country and in the maintenance of justice among nations. Protect them in the hour of danger. Grant that wherever they serve they may be loyal to their high traditions and that at all times they may put their trust in thee; through Jesus Christ our Lord. *Amen.*

## For the Coast Guard

O Lord, who of old didst still the raging of the sea, watch over, we beseech thee, the men of the Coast Guard as they sail upon their missions of helpfulness and succour. Grant them courage and skill and a safe return, and a grateful sense of thy mercy toward them; through the same Jesus Christ our Lord. *Amen.*

## For the Merchant Marine

Almighty God, who raiseth the wind and who maketh the storm a calm, we pray thee for thy blessing upon the seamen of the Merchant Marine, Grant that they that go down to the sea in ships, that do business in great waters, may see thy works, O Lord, and thy wonders in the deep. Preserve them from all peril, both of body and of soul, both at sea and ashore; and give them a heart to praise thy holy name; through Jesus Christ our Lord. *Amen.*

## For Chaplains in the Armed Forces

Blessed Lord, who didst commission thy disciples to continue the work which the Father sent thee into the world to do, support, we beseech thee, with thy Holy Spirit, those who minister in the Armed Forces of our country. Give them grace that they may both by their life and doctrine, set forth thy true and lively word, and rightly and duly administer thy holy sacraments. Strengthen them in their temptations and make them courageous in the perils of their calling, that they may glorify thee before all men; and do thou hold them ever in thy gracious keeping; through Jesus Christ our Lord. *Amen.*

### For Those who Minister to the Wounded and Sick

O merciful God, whose blessed Son went about doing good; Uphold with thy strength and grace those who do service to the wounded and the sick; grant to the ministers of thy gospel faithfulness and love, to the physicians and surgeons wisdom and skill, to the nurses sympathy and patience; and we beseech thee to protect and bless them in all dangers, anxieties, and labours; through Jesus Christ our Lord. *Amen.*

### For the President of the United States, and all in Civil Authority

Almighty God, whose kingdom is everlasting and power infinite; Have mercy upon this whole land; and so rule the hearts of thy servants THE PRESIDENT OF THE UNITED STATES, *The Governor of this State,* and all others in authority, that they, knowing whose ministers they are, may above all things seek thy honour and glory: and that we and all the People, duly considering whose authority they bear, may faithfully and obediently honour them, according to thy blessed Word and ordinance; through Jesus Christ our Lord, who with thee and the Holy Ghost liveth and reigneth ever, one God, world without end. *Amen.*

### For Those in Authority

O Lord God Almighty, guide, we pray thee, all those to whom thou hast committed the government of this nation, and grant to them at this time special gifts of wisdom and understanding, of counsel and strength; that upholding what is right, and following what is true, they may obey thy holy will and fulfil thy divine purpose; through Jesus Christ our Lord. *Amen.*

## FOR JUSTICE AND FREEDOM

O God, the King of righteousness, lead us, we pray thee, in ways of justice and peace; inspire us to break down all tyranny and oppression, to gain for every man his due reward, and from every man his due service; that each may live for all and all may care for each, in Jesus Christ our Lord. *Amen.*

## IN TIME OF WAR

O God, who seest that in this warfare we are seeking to serve thee, and yet in the waging of it must needs do many things that are an offence against thy love, because of the frailty of our nature. Accept we pray thee, our imperfect offering. Arm us with thy Spirit that our warfare may further the victory of thy justice and truth; through Jesus Christ our Lord. *Amen.*

## FOR WORLD PEACE

Almighty God, from whom all thoughts of truth and peace proceed; Kindle, we pray thee, in the hearts of all men the true love of peace, and guide with thy strong and peaceful wisdom those who take counsel for the nations of the earth, that in tranquillity thy kingdom may go forward, till the earth shall be filled with the knowledge of thy love; through Jesus Christ our Lord. *Amen.*

O God, who hast made of one blood all nations of men for to dwell on the face of the whole earth, and didst send thy blessed Son to preach peace to them that are far off and to them that are nigh; Grant that all men everywhere may seek after thee and find thee. Guide, we beseech thee, the Nations of the world into the way of justice and truth, and establish among them that peace which is the fruit of righteousness, that they may become the Kingdom of our Lord and Saviour Jesus Christ. *Amen.*

Eternal God, in whose perfect kingdom no sword is drawn but the sword of righteousness, and no strength known but the strength of love; So guide and inspire, we pray thee, the work of all who seek thy kingdom, that the nations may find their security not in force of arms but in that perfect love which casteth out fear, and in that fellowship revealed to us by thy Son, Jesus Christ our Lord. *Amen.*

## FOR A WILL TO PEACE

Almighty God, by whose grace we look for the day when nation shall not any more lift up sword against nation, and when men shall live without fear in security and peace, grant to us in this time of strife the will to labor for peace even while our sword is drawn to resist the oppressor. Let not the evil we oppose turn us from our purpose to achieve unity and concord among the nations of the earth, to thy honor and glory; through Jesus Christ our Lord. *Amen.*

## FOR THE UNITED NATIONS

Almighty God, we pray thee to guide by thy Holy Spirit the Council and the Assembly of the United Nations. Give to them a right judgment in all things, and the will to seek not only the welfare of their own people, but the greater good of the security and peace and unity of all mankind, that so thy Kingdom may be advanced in the earth; through Jesus Christ our Lord. *Amen.*

## FOR THE WOUNDED

O Lord, we pray thee to have mercy upon all who are this day wounded and suffering. Though kindred and friends be far away, let thy grace be their comfort. Raise them to health again, if it be thy good pleasure; but chiefly give them patience and faith in thee; through Jesus Christ our Lord. *Amen.*

## FOR THOSE IN MENTAL DARKNESS

O Heavenly Father, we beseech thee to have mercy upon all thy children who are living in mental darkness. Restore them to strength of mind and cheerfulness of spirit, and give them health and peace; through Jesus Christ our Lord. *Amen.*

## FOR PRISONERS

We beseech thee, O God, for all prisoners and captives, and all who suffer from oppression, that thou wilt manifest thy mercy toward them, and make the heart of man merciful as thine own, through Jesus Christ our Lord. *Amen.*

## FOR THE LONELY

Have compassion, O most merciful Lord, on all who are lonely and desolate. Be thou their Comforter and Friend; give them such earthly solace as thou seest to be best for them; and bring them to the fuller knowledge of thy love; for the sake of Jesus Christ our Lord. *Amen.*

## FOR THE PERSECUTED

O blessed Lord, who thyself didst undergo the pain and suffering of the Cross; Uphold, we beseech thee, with thy promised gift of strength all those of our brethren who are suffering for their faith in thee. Grant that in the midst of all persecutions they may hold fast by this faith, and that from their stedfastness thy Church may grow in grace and we ourselves in perseverance, to the honor of thy Name, who with the Father and the Holy Ghost art one God, world without end. *Amen.*

## FOR THE DYING

Unto God's gracious mercy and protection we commit you. The Lord bless you and keep you. The Lord make his face to shine upon you, and be gracious unto you. The Lord lift up his countenance upon you, and give you peace, both now and evermore. *Amen.*

## FOR ONE DEPARTED

Almighty God, we remember this day before thee thy faithful servant (*N.*), and we pray thee that, having opened to *him* the gates of larger life, thou wilt receive *him* more and more into thy joyful service; that *he* may win, with thee and thy servants everywhere, the eternal victory; through Jesus Christ our Lord. *Amen.*

## FOR THOSE WHO MOURN

Almighty God, who didst offer thy only Son to be made perfect through suffering, and to win our salvation by enduring the cross; sustain with thy healing power all those whose loved ones have given their lives in the service of our country. Redeem, we pray thee, the pain of their bereavement, that knowing their loss to be the price of our freedom, they may remember the gratitude of the nation for which they gave so costly a sacrifice. And grant, O Lord, that these dead shall not have died in vain, and that out of the distress of this present age there may arise a new and better world in which thy will shall rule, to the honor of thy Son, our Saviour Jesus Christ. *Amen.*

## FOR OUR ENEMIES

O Saviour of the world, our Redeemer, whose love embraces all mankind, we hear thy prayer from the Cross: "Father, forgive them, for they know not what they do." Forgive, O Lord, those who have poured out the innocent blood and caused suffering in the world. May our prayers be for them a ministry of reconciliation. We ask it in thine own Name. *Amen.*

## BENEDICTIONS

The grace of our Lord Jesus Christ, and the love of God, and the fellowship of the Holy Ghost, be with us evermore. *Amen.*

The Lord bless us and keep us. The Lord make his face to shine upon us, and be gracious unto us. The Lord lift up his countenance upon us, and give us peace, this night and evermore. *Amen.*

---

## FOR THOSE AT HOME

Into thy hands, O Father, I commend this day *(this night)* my home, my family, and all who are

dear to me. Bless them with the knowledge of thy
continual presence, uphold them in all cares and
trials, sustain them with thy power; and grant that,
drawing nearer to thee and to each other, we may
ever rejoice in the fellowship of those who trust in
thy goodness and thy love; through Jesus Christ our
Lord. *Amen.*

# Psalms

## PSALM 1

1 Blessed *is* the man that walketh not in the counsel of the ungodly, nor standeth in the way of sinners, nor sitteth in the seat of the scornful.

2 But his delight *is* in the law of the LORD; and in his law doth he meditate day and night.

3 And he shall be like a tree planted by the rivers of water, that bringeth forth his fruit in his season; his leaf also shall not wither; and whatsoever he doeth shall prosper.

4 The ungodly *are* not so: but *are* like the chaff which the wind driveth away.

5 Therefore the ungodly shall not stand in the judgment, nor sinners in the congregation of the righteous.

6 For the LORD knoweth the way of the righteous: but the way of the ungodly shall perish.

## PSALM 15

1 LORD, who shall abide in thy tabernacle? who shall dwell in thy holy hill?

2 He that walketh uprightly, and worketh righteousness, and speaketh the truth in his heart.

3 *He that* backbiteth not with his tongue, nor doeth evil to his neighbour, nor taketh up a reproach against his neighbour.

4 In whose eyes a vile person is contemned; but he honoureth them that fear the LORD. *He that* sweareth to *his own* hurt, and changeth not.

5 *He that* putteth not out his money to usury, nor taketh reward against the innocent. He that doeth these *things* shall never be moved.

## PSALM 19

1 The heavens declare the glory of God; and the firmament sheweth his handywork.

2 Day unto day uttereth speech, and night unto night sheweth knowledge.

3 *There is* no speech nor language, *where* their voice is not heard.

4 Their line is gone out through all the earth, and their words to the end of the world. In them hath he set a tabernacle for the sun,

5 Which *is* as a bridegroom coming out of his chamber, *and* rejoiceth as a strong man to run a race.

6 His going forth *is* from the end of the heaven, and his circuit unto the ends of it: and there is nothing hid from the heat thereof.

7 The law of the LORD *is* perfect, converting the soul: the testimony of the LORD *is* sure, making wise the simple.

8 The statutes of the LORD *are* right, rejoicing the heart: the commandment of the LORD *is* pure, enlightening the eyes.

9 The fear of the LORD *is* clean, enduring for ever: the judgments of the LORD *are* true *and* righteous altogether.

10 More to be desired *are they* than gold, yea, than much fine gold: sweeter also than honey and the honeycomb.

11 Moreover by them is thy servant warned: *and* in keeping of them *there is* great reward.

12 Who can understand *his* errors? cleanse thou me from secret *faults.*

13 Keep back thy servant also from presumptuous *sins;* let them not have dominion over me: then shall

I be upright, and I shall be innocent from the great transgression.

14 Let the words of my mouth, and the meditation of my heart, be acceptable in thy sight, O LORD, my strength, and my redeemer.

## PSALM 23

1 The LORD *is* my shepherd; I shall not want.

2 He maketh me to lie down in green pastures: he leadeth me beside the still waters.

3 He restoreth my soul: he leadeth me in the paths of righteousness for his name's sake.

4 Yea, though I walk through the valley of the shadow of death, I will fear no evil: for thou *art* with me; thy rod and thy staff they comfort me.

5 Thou preparest a table before me in the presence of mine enemies: thou anointest my head with oil; my cup runneth over.

6 Surely goodness and mercy shall follow me all the days of my life: and I will dwell in the house of the LORD for ever.

## PSALM 43

1 Judge me, O God, and plead my cause against an ungodly nation: O deliver me from the deceitful and unjust man.

2 For thou *art* the God of my strength: why dost thou cast me off? why go I mourning because of the oppression of the enemy?

3 O send out thy light and thy truth: let them lead me; let them bring me unto thy holy hill, and to thy tabernacles.

4 Then will I go unto the altar of God, unto God my exceeding joy: yea, upon the harp will I praise thee, O God my God.

5 Why art thou cast down, O my soul? and why art thou disquieted within me? hope in God: for I shall yet praise him, *who is* the health of my countenance, and my God.

## PSALM 46

1 God *is* our refuge and strength, a very present help in trouble.

2 Therefore will not we fear, though the earth be removed, and though the mountains be carried into the midst of the sea;

3 *Though* the waters thereof roar *and* be troubled, *though* the mountains shake with the swelling thereof.

4 *There is* a river, the streams whereof shall make glad the city of God, the holy *place* of the tabernacles of the most High.

5 God *is* in the midst of her; she shall not be moved: God shall help her, *and that* right early.

6 The heathen raged, the kingdoms were moved: he uttered his voice, the earth melted.

7 The LORD of hosts *is* with us; the God of Jacob *is* our refuge.

8 Come, behold the works of the LORD, what desolations he hath made in the earth.

9 He maketh wars to cease unto the end of the earth; he breaketh the bow, and cutteth the spear in sunder; he burneth the chariot in the fire.

10 Be still, and know that I *am* God: I will be exalted among the heathen, I will be exalted in the earth.

11 The LORD of hosts *is* with us; the God of Jacob *is* our refuge.

## PSALM 51

1 Have mercy upon me, O God, according to thy lovingkindness: according unto the multitude of thy tender mercies blot out my transgressions.

2 Wash me thoroughly from mine iniquity, and cleanse me from my sin.

3 For I acknowledge my transgressions: and my sin *is* ever before me.

4 Against thee, thee only, have I sinned, and done *this* evil in thy sight: that thou mightest be justified when thou speakest, *and* be clear when thou judgest.

5 Behold, I was shapen in iniquity; and in sin did my mother conceive me.

6 Behold, thou desirest truth in the inward parts: and in the hidden *part* thou shalt make me to know wisdom.

7 Purge me with hyssop, and I shall be clean: wash me, and I shall be whiter than snow.

8 Make me to hear joy and gladness; *that* the bones *which* thou hast broken may rejoice.

9 Hide thy face from my sins, and blot out all mine iniquities.

10 Create in me a clean heart, O God; and renew a right spirit within me.

11 Cast me not away from thy presence; and take not thy holy spirit from me.

12 Restore unto me the joy of thy salvation; and uphold me *with thy* free spirit.

13 *Then* will I teach transgressors thy ways; and sinners shall be converted unto thee.

14 Deliver me from bloodguiltiness, O God, thou God of my salvation: *and* my tongue shall sing aloud of thy righteousness.

15 O Lord, open thou my lips: and my mouth shall shew forth thy praise.

16 For thou desirest not sacrifice; else would I give *it*: thou delightest not in burnt offering.

17 The sacrifices of God *are* a broken spirit: a broken and contrite heart, O God, thou wilt not despise.

18 Do good in thy good pleasure unto Zion: build thou the walls of Jerusalem.

19 Then shalt thou be pleased with the sacrifices of righteousness, with burnt offering and whole burnt offering: then shall they offer bullocks upon thine altar.

## Psalm 72

1 Give the king thy judgments, O God, and thy righteousness unto the king's son.

2 He shall judge thy people with righteousness, and thy poor with judgment.

3 The mountains shall bring peace to the people, and the little hills, by righteousness.

4 He shall judge the poor of the people, he shall save the children of the needy, and shall break in pieces the oppressor.

5 They shall fear thee as long as the sun and moon endure, throughout all generations.

6 He shall come down like rain upon the mown grass: as showers *that* water the earth.

7 In his days shall the righteous flourish; and abundance of peace so long as the moon endureth.

8 He shall have dominion also from sea to sea, and from the river unto the ends of the earth.

9 They that dwell in the wilderness shall bow before him; and his enemies shall lick the dust.

10 The kings of Tarshish and of the isles shall bring presents: the kings of Sheba and Seba shall offer gifts.

11 Yea, all kings shall fall down before him: all nations shall serve him.

12 For he shall deliver the needy when he crieth; the poor also, and *him* that hath no helper.

13 He shall spare the poor and needy, and shall save the souls of the needy.

14 He shall redeem their soul from deceit and violence: and precious shall their blood be in his sight.

15 And he shall live, and to him shall be given of the gold of Sheba: prayer also shall be made for him continually; *and* daily shall he be praised.

16 There shall be an handful of corn in the earth upon the top of the mountains; the fruit thereof shall shake like Lebanon: and *they* of the city shall flourish like grass of the earth.

17 His name shall endure for ever: his name shall be continued as long as the sun: and *men* shall be blessed in him: All nations shall call him blessed.

18 Blessed *be* the LORD God, the God of Israel, who only doeth wondrous things.

19 And blessed *be* his glorious name for ever: and let the whole earth be filled *with* his glory; A-men, and A-men.

## PSALM 84

1 How amiable *are* thy tabernacles, O LORD of hosts!

2 My soul longeth, yea, even fainteth for the courts of the LORD: my heart and my flesh crieth out for the living God.

3 Yea, the sparrow hath found an house, and the

swallow a nest for herself, where she may lay her young, *even* thine altars, O LORD of hosts, my King, and my God.

4 Blessed *are* they that dwell in thy house: they will be still praising thee.

5 Blessed *is* the man whose strength *is* in thee; in whose heart *are* the ways *of them.*

6 *Who* passing through the valley of Baca make it a well; the rain also filleth the pools.

7 They go from strength to strength, *every one of them* in Zion appeareth before God.

8 O LORD God of hosts, hear my prayer: give ear, O God of Jacob.

9 Behold, O God our shield, and look upon the face of thine anointed.

10 For a day in thy courts *is* better than a thousand. I had rather be a doorkeeper in the house of my God, than to dwell in the tents of wickedness.

11 For the LORD God *is* a sun and shield: the LORD will give grace and glory: no good *thing* will he withhold from them that walk uprightly.

12 O LORD of hosts, blessed *is* the man that trusteth in thee.

## PSALM 91

1 He that dwelleth in the secret place of the most High shall abide under the shadow of the Almighty.

2 I will say of the LORD, *He is* my refuge and my fortress: my God; in him will I trust.

3 Surely he shall deliver thee from the snare of the fowler, *and* from the noisome pestilence.

4 He shall cover thee with his feathers, and under his wings shalt thou trust: his truth *shall be thy* shield and buckler.

5 Thou shalt not be afraid for the terror by night; *nor* for the arrow *that* flieth by day;

6 *Nor* for the pestilence *that* walketh in darkness; *nor* for the destruction *that* wasteth at noonday.

7 A thousand shall fall at thy side, and ten thousand at thy right hand; *but* it shall not come nigh thee.

8 Only with thine eyes shalt thou behold and see the reward of the wicked.

9 Because thou hast made the LORD, *which is* my refuge, *even* the most High, thy habitation;

10 There shall no evil befall thee, neither shall any plague come nigh thy dwelling.

11 For he shall give his angels charge over thee, to keep thee in all thy ways.

12 They shall bear thee up in *their* hands, lest thou dash thy foot against a stone.

13 Thou shalt tread upon the lion and adder: the young lion and the dragon shalt thou trample under feet.

14 Because he hath set his love upon me, therefore will I deliver him: I will set him on high, because he hath known my name.

15 He shall call upon me, and I will answer him: I *will be* with him in trouble; I will deliver him, and honour him.

16 With long life will I satisfy him, and shew him my salvation.

## PSALM 95

1 O come, let us sing unto the LORD: let us make a joyful noise to the rock of our salvation.

2 Let us come before his presence with thanksgiving, and make a joyful noise unto him with psalms.

3 For the LORD *is* a great God, and a great King above all gods.

4 In his hand *are* the deep places of the earth: the strength of the hills *is* his also.

5 The sea *is* his, and he made it: and his hands formed the dry *land*.

6 O come, let us worship and bow down: let us kneel before the LORD our maker.

7 For he *is* our God; and we *are* the people of his pasture, and the sheep of his hand. To day if ye will hear his voice,

8 Harden not your heart, as in the provocation, *and* as *in* the day of temptation in the wilderness:

9 When your fathers tempted me, proved me, and saw my work.

10 Forty years long was I grieved with *this* generation, and said, It *is* a people that do err in their heart, and they have not known my ways:

11 Unto whom I sware in my wrath that they should not enter into my rest.

## PSALM 96

1 O sing unto the LORD a new song: sing unto the LORD, all the earth.

2 Sing unto the LORD, bless his name; shew forth his salvation from day to day.

3 Declare his glory among the heathen, his wonders among all people.

4 For the LORD *is* great, and greatly to be praised: he *is* to be feared above all gods.

5 For all the gods of the nations *are* idols: but the LORD made the heavens.

6 Honour and majesty *are* before him: strength and beauty *are* in his sanctuary.

7 Give unto the LORD, O ye kindreds of the people, give unto the LORD glory and strength.

8 Give unto the LORD the glory *due unto* his name: bring an offering, and come into his courts.

9 O worship the LORD in the beauty of holiness: fear before him, all the earth.

10 Say among the heathen *that* the LORD reigneth: the world also shall be established that it shall not be moved: he shall judge the people righteously.

11 Let the heavens rejoice, and let the earth be glad; let the sea roar, and the fulness thereof.

12 Let the field be joyful, and all that *is* therein: then shall all the trees of the wood rejoice

13 Before the LORD: for he cometh, for he cometh to judge the earth: he shall judge the world with righteousness, and the people with his truth.


## PSALM 100

1 Make a joyful noise unto the LORD, all ye lands.

2 Serve the LORD with gladness: come before his presence with singing.

3 Know ye that the LORD he *is* God: *it is* he *that* hath made us, and not we ourselves; *we are* his people, and the sheep of his pasture.

4 Enter into his gates with thanksgiving, *and* into his courts with praise: be thankful unto him, *and* bless his name.

5 For the LORD *is* good; his mercy *is* everlasting; and his truth *endureth* to all generations.


## PSALM 103

1 Bless the LORD, O my soul: and all that is within me, *bless* his holy name.

2 Bless the LORD, O my soul, and forget not all his benefits:

3 Who forgiveth all thine iniquities; who healeth all thy diseases;

4 Who redeemeth thy life from destruction; who crowneth thee with lovingkindness and tender mercies;

5 Who satisfieth thy mouth with good *things; so that* thy youth is renewed like the eagle's.

6 The LORD executeth righteousness and judgment for all that are oppressed.

7 He made known his ways unto Moses, his acts unto the children of Israel.

8 The LORD *is* merciful and gracious, slow to anger, and plenteous in mercy.

9 He will not always chide: neither will he keep *his anger* for ever.

10 He hath not dealt with us after our sins; nor rewarded us according to our iniquities.

11 For as the heaven is high above the earth, *so* great is his mercy toward them that fear him.

12 As far as the east is from the west, *so* far hath he removed our transgressions from us.

13 Like as a father pitieth *his* children, *so* the LORD pitieth them that fear him.

14 For he knoweth our frame; he remembereth that we *are* dust.

15 *As for* man, his days *are* as grass: as a flower of the field, so he flourisheth.

16 For the wind passeth over it, and it is gone; and the place thereof shall know it no more.

17 But the mercy of the LORD *is* from everlasting to everlasting upon them that fear him, and his righteousness unto children's children;

18 To such as keep his covenant, and to those that remember his commandments to do them.

19 The LORD hath prepared his throne in the heavens; and his kingdom ruleth over all.

20 Bless the LORD, ye his angels, that excel in strength, that do his commandments, hearkening unto the voice of his word.

21 Bless ye the LORD, all *ye* his hosts: *ye* ministers of his, that do his pleasure.

22 Bless the LORD, all his works in all places of his dominion: bless the LORD, O my soul.

## PSALM 119

9 Wherewithal shall a young man cleanse his way? by taking heed *thereto* according to thy word.

10 With my whole heart have I sought thee: O let me not wander from thy commandments.

11 Thy word have I hid in mine heart, that I might not sin against thee.

12 Blessed *art* thou, O LORD: teach me thy statutes.

13 With my lips have I declared all the judgments of thy mouth.

14 I have rejoiced in the way of thy testimonies, as *much as* in all riches.

15 I will meditate in thy precepts, and have respect unto thy ways.

16 I will delight myself in thy statutes: I will not forget thy word.

## PSALM 121

1 I will lift up mine eyes unto the hills, from whence cometh my help.

2 My help *cometh* from the LORD, which made heaven and earth.

3 He will not suffer thy foot to be moved; he that keepeth thee will not slumber.

4 Behold, he that keepeth Israel shall neither slumber nor sleep.

5 The LORD *is* thy keeper: the LORD *is* thy shade upon thy right hand.

6 The sun shall not smite thee by day, nor the moon by night.

7 The LORD shall preserve thee from all evil: he shall preserve thy soul.

8 The LORD shall preserve thy going out and thy coming in from this time forth, and even for evermore.

## PSALM 124

1 If *it had not been* the LORD who was on our side, now may Israel say;

2 If *it had not been* the LORD who was on our side, when men rose up against us:

3 Then they had swallowed us up quick, when their wrath was kindled against us:

4 Then the waters had overwhelmed us, the stream had gone over our soul:

5 Then the proud waters had gone over our soul.

6 Blessed *be* the LORD, who hath not given us *as* a prey to their teeth.

7 Our soul is escaped as a bird out of the snare of the fowlers: the snare is broken, and we are escaped.

8 Our help *is* in the name of the LORD, who made heaven and earth.

## PSALM 130

1 Out of the depths have I cried unto thee, O LORD.

2 LORD, hear my voice: let thine ears be attentive to the voice of my supplications.

3 If thou, LORD, shouldest mark iniquities, O LORD, who shall stand?

4 But *there* is forgiveness with thee, that thou mayest be feared.

5 I wait for the LORD, my soul doth wait, and in his word do I hope.

6 My soul *waiteth* for the Lord more than they that watch for the morning: I *say, more than* they that watch for the morning.

7 Let Israel hope in the LORD: for with the LORD *there is* mercy, and with him *is* plenteous redemption.

8 And he shall redeem Israel from all his iniquities.

## PSALM 150

1 Praise ye the LORD. Praise God in his sanctuary: praise him in the firmament of his power.

2 Praise him for his mighty acts: praise him according to his excellent greatness.

3 Praise him with the sound of the trumpet: praise him with the psaltery and harp.

4 Praise him with the timbrel and dance: praise him with stringed instruments and organs.

5 Praise him upon the loud cymbals; praise him upon the high sounding cymbals.

6 Let every thing that hath breath praise the LORD. Praise ye the LORD.

# Bible Readings

Come now, and let us reason together, saith the LORD: though your sins be as scarlet, they shall be as white as snow; though they be red like crimson, they shall be as wool. *Isaiah* 1:18

Fear thou not; for I *am* with thee: be not dismayed; for I *am* thy God: I will strengthen thee; yea, I will help thee; yea, I will uphold thee with the right hand of my righteousness. *Isaiah* 41:10

Look unto me, and be ye saved, all the ends of the earth: for I *am* God, and *there is* none else. *Isaiah* 45:22

He hath shewed thee, O man, what *is* good; and what doth the LORD require of thee, but to do justly, and to love mercy, and to walk humbly with thy God? *Micah* 6:8

For the Son of man is come to seek and to save that which was lost. *Luke* 19:10

This *is* a faithful saying, and worthy of all acceptation, that Christ Jesus came into the world to save sinners; of whom I am chief. *I Timothy* 1:15

28 Come unto me, all *ye* that labour and are heavy laden, and I will give you rest.

29 Take my yoke upon you, and learn of me; for I am meek and lowly in heart: and ye shall find rest unto your souls.

30 For my yoke *is* easy, and my burden is light. *Matthew* 11:28–30

9 I am the door: by me if any man enter in, he shall be saved, and shall go in and out, and find pasture.

10 The thief cometh not, but for to steal, and to kill, and to destroy: I am come that they might have life, and that they might have *it* more abundantly.

11 I am the good shepherd: the good shepherd giveth his life for the sheep. *John* 10:9-11

1 Let not your heart be troubled: ye believe in God, believe also in me.

2 In my Father's house are many mansions: if *it were* not *so*, I would have told you. I go to prepare a place for you.

3 And if I go and prepare a place for you, I will come again, and receive you unto myself; that where I am, *there* ye may be also.

4 And whither I go ye know, and the way ye know. *John* 14:1-4

23 But the hour cometh, and now is, when the true worshippers shall worship the Father in spirit and in truth: for the Father seeketh such to worship him.

24 God *is* a Spirit: and they that worship him must worship *him* in spirit and in truth. *John* 4:23,24

12 This is my commandment, That ye love one another, as I have loved you.

13 Greater love hath no man than this, that a man lay down his life for his friends. *John* 15:12,13

33 These things I have spoken unto you, that in me ye might have peace. In the world ye shall have tribulation: but be of good cheer; I have overcome the world. *John* 16:33

## More than Conquerors

35 Who shall separate us from the love of Christ? *shall* tribulation, or distress, or persecution, or famine, or nakedness, or peril, or sword?

36 As it is written, For thy sake we are killed all the day long; we are accounted as sheep for the slaughter.

37 Nay, in all these things we are more than conquerors through him that loved us.

38 For I am persuaded, that neither death, nor life, nor angels, nor principalities, nor powers, nor things present, nor things to come,

39 Nor height, nor depth, nor any other creature, shall be able to separate us from the love of God, which is in Christ Jesus our Lord. *Romans* 8:35-39

## STRENGTH FROM GOD

28 Hast thou not known? hast thou not heard *that* the everlasting God, the LORD, the Creator of the ends of the earth, fainteth not, neither is weary? *there is* no searching of his understanding.

29 He giveth power to the faint; and to *them that have* no might he increaseth strength.

30 Even the youths shall faint and be weary, and the young men shall utterly fall:

31 But they that wait upon the LORD shall renew *their* strength; they shall mount up with wings as eagles; they shall run, and not be weary; *and* they shall walk, and not faint. *Isaiah* 40:28-31

## THE PRIZE-WINNER

24 Know ye not that they which run in a race run all, but one receiveth the prize? So run, that ye may obtain. *I Corinthians* 9:24.

25 And every man that striveth for the mastery is temperate in all things. Now they *do it* to obtain a corruptible crown; but we an incorruptible.

26 I therefore so run, not as uncertainly; so fight I, not as one that beateth the air:

27 But I keep under my body, and bring *it* into subjection: lest that by any means, when I have preached to others, I myself should be a castaway. *I Corinthians* 9:24–27

## THE PEACE OF GOD

4 Rejoice in the Lord alway: *and* again I say, Rejoice.

5 Let your moderation be known unto all men. The Lord *is* at hand.

6 Be careful for nothing; but in every thing by prayer and supplication with thanksgiving let your requests be made known unto God.

7 And the peace of God, which passeth all understanding, shall keep your hearts and minds through Christ Jesus.

8 Finally, brethren, whatsoever things are true, whatsoever things *are* honest, whatsoever things *are* just, whatsoever things *are* pure, whatsoever things *are* lovely, whatsoever things *are* of good report; if *there be* any virtue, and if *there be* any praise, think on these things. *Philippians* 4:4–8

## THE BEATITUDES

1 And seeing the multitudes, he went up into a mountain: and when he was set, his disciples came unto him:

2 And he opened his mouth, and taught them, saying,

3 Blessed *are* the poor in spirit: for their's is the kingdom of heaven.

4 Blessed *are* they that mourn: for they shall be comforted.

5 Blessed *are* the meek: for they shall inherit the earth.

6 Blessed *are* they which do hunger and thirst after righteousness: for they shall be filled.

7 Blessed *are* the merciful: for they shall obtain mercy.

8 Blessed *are* the pure in heart: for they shall see God.

9 Blessed *are* the peacemakers: for they shall be called the children of God.

10 Blessed *are* they which are persecuted for righteousness' sake: for their's is the kingdom of heaven.

11 Blessed are ye, when *men* shall revile you, and persecute *you*, and shall say all manner of evil against you falsely, for my sake.

12 Rejoice, and be exceeding glad: for great *is* your reward in heaven: for so persecuted they the prophets which were before you.

13 Ye are the salt of the earth: but if the salt have lost his savour, wherewith shall it be salted? it is thenceforth good for nothing, but to be cast out, and to be trodden under foot of men.

14 Ye are the light of the world. A city that is set on an hill cannot be hid.

15 Neither do men light a candle, and put it under a bushel, but on a candlestick; and it giveth light unto all that are in the house.

16 Let your light so shine before men, that they may see your good works, and glorify your Father which is in heaven. *Matthew* 5:1-16

PRAYER

5 And when thou prayest, thou shalt not be as the hypocrites *are:* for they love to pray standing in the synagogues and in the corners of the streets, that they may be seen of men. Verily I say unto you, They have their reward.

6 But thou, when thou prayest, enter into thy closet, and when thou hast shut thy door, pray to thy Father which is in secret; and thy Father which seeth in secret shall reward thee openly.

7 But when ye pray, use not vain repetitions, as the heathen *do:* for they think that they shall be heard for their much speaking.

8 Be not ye therefore like unto them: for your Father knoweth what things ye have need of, before ye ask him.

9 After this manner therefore pray ye: Our Father which art in heaven, Hallowed be thy name.

10 Thy kingdom come. Thy will be done in earth, as *it is* in heaven.

11 Give us this day our daily bread.

12 And forgive us our debts, as we forgive our debtors.

13 And lead us not into temptation, but deliver us from evil: For thine is the kingdom, and the power, and the glory, for ever. Amen.

14 For if ye forgive men their trespasses, your heavenly Father will also forgive you:

15 But if ye forgive not men their trespasses, neither will your Father forgive your trespasses.

*Matthew* 6:5–12

THE FATHER'S KINGDOM

25 Therefore I say unto you, Take no thought for your life, what ye shall eat, or what ye shall drink;

nor yet for your body, what ye shall put on. Is not the life more than meat, and the body than raiment?

26 Behold the fowls of the air: for they sow not, neither do they reap, nor gather into barns; yet your heavenly Father feedeth them. Are ye not much better than they?

27 Which of you by taking thought can add one cubit unto his stature?

28 And why take ye thought for raiment? Consider the lilies of the field, how they grow; they toil not, neither do they spin:

29 And yet I say unto you, That even Solomon in all his glory was not arrayed like one of these.

30 Wherefore, if God so clothe the grass of the field, which to day is, and to morrow is cast into the oven, *shall he* not much more *clothe* you, O ye of little faith?

31 Therefore take no thought, saying, What shall we eat? or, What shall we drink? or, Wherewithal shall we be clothed?

32 (For after all these things do the Gentiles seek:) for your heavenly Father knoweth that ye have need of all these things.

33 But seek ye first the kingdom of God, and his righteousness; and all these things shall be added unto you.

34 Take therefore no thought for the morrow: for the morrow shall take thought for the things of itself. Sufficient unto the day *is* the evil thereof. *Matthew* 6:25-34

## THE PRODIGAL SON

11 And he said, A certain man had two sons:

12 And the younger of them said to *his* father,

Father, give me the portion of goods that falleth *to me*. And he divided unto them *his* living.

13 And not many days after the younger son gathered all together, and took his journey into a far country, and there wasted his substance with riotous living.

14 And when he had spent all, there arose a mighty famine in that land; and he began to be in want.

15 And he went and joined himself to a citizen of that country; and he sent him into his fields to feed swine.

16 And he would fain have filled his belly with the husks that the swine did eat: and no man gave unto him.

17 And when he came to himself, he said, How many hired servants of my father's have bread enough and to spare, and I perish with hunger!

18 I will arise and go to my father, and will say unto him, Father, I have sinned against heaven, and before thee,

19 And am no more worthy to be called thy son: make me as one of thy hired servants.

20 And he arose, and came to his father. But when he was yet a great way off, his father saw him, and had compassion, and ran, and fell on his neck, and kissed him.

21 And the son said unto him, Father, I have sinned against heaven, and in thy sight, and am no more worthy to be called thy son.

22 But the father said to his servants, Bring forth the best robe, and put *it* on him; and put a ring on his hand, and shoes on *his* feet:

23 And bring hither the fatted calf, and kill *it;* and let us eat, and be merry:

24 For this my son was dead, and is alive again;

he was lost, and is found. And they began to be merry.
*Luke* 15:11-24

## THE PHARISEE AND THE PUBLICAN

9 And he spake this parable unto certain which trusted in themselves that they were righteous, and despised others:

10 Two men went up into the temple to pray; the one a Pharisee, and the other a publican.

11 The Pharisee stood and prayed thus with himself, God, I thank thee, that I am not as other men *are*, extortioners, unjust, adulterers, or even as this publican.

12 I fast twice in the week, I give tithes of all that I possess.

13 And the publican, standing afar off, would not lift up so much as *his* eyes unto heaven, but smote upon his breast, saying, God be merciful to me a sinner.

14 I tell you, this man went down to his house justified *rather* than the other: for every one that exalteth himself shall be abased; and he that humbleth himself shall be exalted. *Luke* 18:9-14

## THE SAVIOUR OF THE WORLD

16 For God so loved the world, that he gave his only begotten Son, that whosoever believeth in him should not perish, but have everlasting life.

17 For God sent not his Son into the world to condemn the world; but that the world through him might be saved.

18 He that believeth on him is not condemned: but he that believeth not is condemned already, because he hath not believed in the name of the only begotten Son of God.

19 And this is the condemnation, that light is come

into the world, and men loved darkness rather than light, because their deeds were evil.

20 For every one that doeth evil hateth the light, neither cometh to the light, lest his deeds should be reproved.

21 But he that doeth truth cometh to the light, that his deeds may be made manifest, that they are wrought in God. *John* 3:16–21

## CHRISTIAN LOVE

1 Though I speak with the tongues of men and of angels, and have not charity, I am become *as* sounding brass, or a tinkling cymbal.

2 And though I have *the gift of* prophecy, and understand all mysteries, and all knowledge; and though I have all faith, so that I could remove mountains, and have not charity, I am nothing.

3 And though I bestow all my goods to feed *the poor*, and though I give my body to be burned, and have not charity, it profiteth me nothing.

4 Charity suffereth long, *and* is kind; charity envieth not; charity vaunteth not itself, is not puffed up,

5 Doth not behave itself unseemly, seeketh not her own, is not easily provoked, thinketh no evil;

6 Rejoiceth not in iniquity, but rejoiceth in the truth;

7 Beareth all things, believeth all things, hopeth all things, endureth all things.

8 Charity never faileth: but whether *there be* prophecies, they shall fail; whether *there be* tongues, they shall cease; whether *there be* knowledge, it shall vanish away.

9 For we know in part, and we prophesy in part.

10 But when that which is perfect is come, then that which is in part shall be done away.

11 When I was a child, I spake as a child, I understood as a child, I thought as a child: but when I became a man, I put away childish things.

12 For now we see through a glass, darkly; but then face to face: now I know in part; but then shall I know even as also I am known.

13 And now abideth faith, hope, charity, these three; but the greatest of these *is* charity. *I Corinthians* 13:1-13

## THE ARMOUR OF GOD

10 Finally, my brethren, be strong in the Lord, and in the power of his might.

11 Put on the whole armour of God, that ye may be able to stand against the wiles of the devil.

12 For we wrestle not against flesh and blood, but against principalities, against powers, against the rulers of the darkness of this world, against spiritual wickedness in high *places*.

13 Wherefore take unto you the whole armour of God, that ye may be able to withstand in the evil day, and having done all, to stand.

14 Stand therefore, having your loins girt about with truth, and having on the breastplate of righteousness;

15 And your feet shod with the preparation of the gospel of peace;

16 Above all, taking the shield of faith, wherewith ye shall be able to quench all the fiery darts of the wicked.

17 And take the helmet of salvation, and the sword of the Spirit, which is the word of God:

18 Praying always with all prayer and supplication in the Spirit, and watching thereunto with all perseverance and supplication for all saints;

19 And for me, that utterance may be given unto me, that I may open my mouth boldly, to make known the mystery of the gospel,

20 For which I am an ambassador in bonds: that therein I may speak boldly, as I ought to speak. *Ephesians* 6:10-20

## THE HIGH CALLING OF GOD

7 But what things were gain to me, those I counted loss for Christ.

8 Yea doubtless, and I count all things *but* loss for the excellency of the knowledge of Christ Jesus my Lord: for whom I have suffered the loss of all things, and do count them *but* dung, that I may win Christ,

9 And be found in him, not having mine own righteousness, which is of the law, but that which is through the faith of Christ, the righteousness which is of God by faith:

10 That I may know him, and the power of his resurrection, and the fellowship of his sufferings, being made conformable unto his death;

11 If by any means I might attain unto the resurrection of the dead.

12 Not as though I had already attained, either were already perfect: but I follow after, if that I may apprehend that for which also I am apprehended of Christ Jesus.

13 Brethren, I count not myself to have apprehended: but *this* one thing *I do*, forgetting those things which are behind, and reaching forth unto those things which are before,

14 I press toward the mark for the prize of the high calling of God in Christ Jesus. *Philippians* 3:7-14

## THE REWARD OF LOYALTY

43 And in the midst of them there was a young man of a high stature, taller than all the rest, and upon every one of their heads he set crowns, and was more exalted; which I marvelled at greatly.

44 So I asked the angel, and said, Sir, what are these?

45 He answered and said unto me, These be they that have put off the mortal clothing, and put on the immortal, and have confessed the name of God: now are they crowned, and receive palms.

46 Then said I unto the angel, What young person is it that crowneth them, and giveth them palms in their hands?

47 So he answered and said unto me, It is the Son of God, whom they have confessed in the world. Then began I greatly to commend them that stood so stiffly for the name of the Lord.

48 Then the angel said unto me, Go thy way, and tell my people what manner of things, and how great wonders of the Lord thy God, thou hast seen. *II Esdras 2:43-48*

## PURE RELIGION

16 Do not err, my beloved brethren.

17 Every good gift and every perfect gift is from above, and cometh down from the Father of lights, with whom is no variableness, neither shadow of turning.

18 Of his own will begat he us with the word of truth, that we should be a kind of firstfruits of his creatures.

19 Wherefore, my beloved brethren, let every man be swift to hear, slow to speak, slow to wrath:

20 For the wrath of man worketh not the righteousness of God.

21 Wherefore lay apart all filthiness and superfluity of naughtiness, and receive with meekness the engrafted word, which is able to save your souls.

22 But be ye doers of the word, and not hearers only, deceiving your own selves.

23 For if any be a hearer of the word, and not a doer, he is like unto a man beholding his natural face in a glass:

24 For he beholdeth himself, and goeth his way, and straightway forgetteth what manner of man he was.

25 For whoso looketh into the perfect law of liberty, and continueth *therein*, he being not a forgetful hearer, but a doer of the work, this man shall be blessed in his deed.

26 If any man among you seem to be religious, and bridleth not his tongue, but deceiveth his own heart, this man's religion *is* vain.

27 Pure religion and undefiled before God and the Father is this, To visit the fatherless and widows in their affliction, *and* to keep himself unspotted from the world. *James* 1:16-27

### THE VISION OF THE FUTURE

9 After this I beheld, and, lo, a great multitude, which no man could number, of all nations, and kindreds, and people, and tongues, stood before the throne, and before the Lamb, clothed with white robes, and palms in their hands;

10 And cried with a loud voice, saying, Salvation to our God which sitteth upon the throne, and unto the Lamb.

11 And all the angels stood round about the throne, and *about* the elders and the four beasts, and fell before the throne on their faces, and worshipped God,

12 Saying, Amen: Blessing, and glory, and wisdom, and thanksgiving, and honour, and power, and might, *be* unto our God for ever and ever. Amen.

13 And one of the elders answered, saying unto me, What are these which are arrayed in white robes? and whence came they?

14 And I said unto him, Sir, thou knowest. And he said to me, These are they which came out of great tribulation, and have washed their robes, and made them white in the blood of the Lamb.

15 Therefore are they before the throne of God, and serve him day and night in his temple: and he that sitteth on the throne shall dwell among them.

16 They shall hunger no more, neither thirst any more; neither shall the sun light on them, nor any heat.

17 For the Lamb which is in the midst of the throne shall feed them, and shall lead them unto living fountains of waters: and God shall wipe away all tears from their eyes. *Revelation* 7:9–17

# Hymns *

**1.**
(3)

1 O saving Victim, opening wide
    The gate of heaven to man below,
Our foes press on from every side,
    Thine aid supply, thy strength bestow.

2 All praise and thanks to thee ascend
    For evermore, blest One in Three;
O grant us life that shall not end,
    In our true native land with thee. **Amen.**

**2.**
(4)

1 I need thee every hour,
    Most gracious Lord;
No tender voice like thine
    Can peace afford.

*I need thee, O I need thee,*
*Every hour I need thee;*
*O bless me now, my Saviour,*
*I come to thee!*

2 I need thee every hour;
    Stay thou near by;
Temptations lose their power
    When thou art nigh.

*I need thee, O I need thee,*
*Every hour I need thee;*
*O bless me now, my Saviour,*
*I come to thee!*

* Numbers in parentheses indicate the number of the hymn in The Wayside Hymnal, published by The Forward Movement, 412 Sycamore Street, Cincinnati 2, Ohio.

3 I need thee every hour,
In joy or pain;
Come quickly and abide,
Or life is vain.

*I need thee, O I need thee,
Every hour I need thee;
O bless me now, my Saviour,
I come to thee!*

4 I need thee every hour;
Teach me thy will;
And thy rich promises
In me fulfil.

*I need thee, O I need thee,
Every hour I need thee;
O bless me now, my Saviour,
I come to thee!*

5 I need thee every hour,
Most Holy One;
O make me thine indeed,
Thou blessed Son!

*I need thee, O I need thee,
Every hour I need thee;
O bless me now, my Saviour,
I come to thee!* Amen.

3.                    (5)

1 Abide with me: fast falls the eventide;
The darkness deepens; Lord, with me abide:
When other helpers fail, and comforts flee,
Help of the helpless, O abide with me.

2 Swift to its close ebbs out life's little day;
Earth's joys grow dim, its glories pass away,
Change and decay in all around I see;
O thou who changest not, abide with me.

3 I need thy presence every passing hour;
What but thy grace can foil the tempter's power?
Who, like thyself, my guide and stay can be?
Through cloud and sunshine, Lord, abide with me.

4 I fear no foe, with thee at hand to bless:
Ills have no weight, and tears no bitterness.
Where is death's sting? where, grave, thy victory?
I triumph still, if thou abide with me.

5 Hold thou thy cross before my closing eyes:
Shine through the gloom, and point me to the skies:
Heaven's morning breaks, and earth's vain shadows
    flee:
In life, in death, O Lord, abide with me. Amen.

**4.**                    (7)

1 Sun of my soul, thou Saviour dear,
    It is not night if thou be near;
    O may no earth-born cloud arise
    To hide thee from thy servant's eyes.

2 When the soft dews of kindly sleep
    My weary eyelids gently steep,
    Be my last thought, how sweet to rest
    For ever on my Saviour's breast.

3 Abide with me from morn till eve,
    For without thee I cannot live;
    Abide with me when night is nigh,
    For without thee I dare not die.

4 If some poor wandering child of thine
　　Have spurned to-day the voice divine,
　　Now, Lord, the gracious work begin;
　　Let him no more lie down in sin.

5 Watch by the sick; enrich the poor
　　With blessings from thy boundless store;
　　Be every mourner's sleep to-night,
　　Like infant's slumbers, pure and light.

6 Come near and bless us when we wake,
　　Ere through the world our way we take,
　　Till in the ocean of thy love
　　We lose ourselves in heaven above. Amen.

**5.** (9)

1 Now the day is over,
　　　Night is drawing nigh,
　　　Shadows of the evening
　　　Steal across the sky.

2 Jesus, give the weary
　　　Calm and sweet repose;
　　　With thy tenderest blessing
　　　May our eyelids close.

3 Grant to little children
　　　Visions bright of thee;
　　　Guard the sailors tossing
　　　On the deep, blue sea.

4 Comfort every sufferer
　　　Watching late in pain;
　　　Those who plan some evil
　　　From their sin restrain.

5 Through the long night watches,
   May thine angels spread
   Their white wings above me,
   Watching round my bed.

6 When the morning wakens,
   Then may I arise
   Pure, and fresh, and sinless
   In thy holy eyes. Amen.

**6.** (11)

1 Guide me, O thou great Jehovah,
   Pilgrim through this barren land,
I am weak, but thou art mighty;
   Hold me with thy powerful hand.

2 Open now the crystal fountains
   Whence the living waters flow;
Let the fiery, cloudy pillar
   Lead me all my journey through.

3 Feed me with the heavenly manna
   In this barren wilderness;
Be my sword, and shield, and banner,
   Be the Lord my Righteousness.

4 When I tread the verge of Jordan,
   Bid my anxious fears subside;
Death of death, and hell's destruction,
   Land me safe on Canaan's side. Amen.

**7.** (16)

1 O little town of Bethlehem,
    How still we see thee lie!
Above thy deep and dreamless sleep
    The silent stars go by;
Yet in thy dark streets shineth
    The everlasting Light;
The hopes and fears of all the years
    Are met in thee to-night.

2 For Christ is born of Mary,
    And gathered all above,
While mortals sleep, the angels keep
    Their watch of wondering love.
O morning stars, together
    Proclaim the holy birth!
And praises sing to God the King,
    And peace to men on earth.

3 How silently, how silently,
    The wondrous gift is given!
So God imparts to human hearts
    The blessings of his heaven.
No ear may hear his coming,
    But in this world of sin,
Where meek souls will receive him, **still**
    The dear Christ enters in.

4 O holy Child of Bethlehem!
    Descend to us, we pray;
Cast out our sin and enter in,
    Be born in us to-day.
We hear the Christmas angels
    The great glad tidings tell;
O come to us, abide with us,
    Our Lord Emmanuel! Amen.

**8.**

### (17)

1    O come, all ye faithful,
      Joyful and triumphant,
O come ye, O come ye to Bethlehem;
    Come and behold him
    Born the King of angels;
    O come, let us adore him,
    O come, let us adore him,
O come, let us adore him, Christ the Lord.

2    God of God,
      Light of Light,
Lo! He abhors not the Virgin's womb:
    Very God,
    Begotten, not created;
    O come, let us adore him, etc.

3    Sing, choirs of angels,
      Sing in exultation,
Sing, all ye citizens of heaven above;
    Glory to God
    In the highest;
    O come, let us adore him, etc.

4    Yea, Lord, we greet thee,
      Born this happy morning;
Jesus, to thee be glory given;
    Word of the Father,
    Now in flesh appearing;
    O come, let us adore him, etc. Amen.

**9.** (19)

1 Silent night, holy night,
All is calm, all is bright
Round yon virgin mother and child.
Holy infant so tender and mild,
Sleep in heavenly peace.

2 Silent night, holy night,
Shepherds quake at the sight,
Glories stream from heaven afar,
Heavenly hosts sing alleluia;
Christ, the Saviour, is born!

3 Silent night, holy night,
Son of God, love's pure light
Radiant beams from thy holy face,
With the dawn of redeeming grace,
Jesus, Lord, at thy birth. Amen.

**10.** (18)

1 How firm a foundation, ye saints of the Lord,
Is laid for your faith in his excellent word!
What more can he say than to you he hath said,
You who unto Jesus for refuge have fled?

2 "Fear not, I am with thee; O be not dismayed!
I, I am thy God, and will still give thee aid;
I'll strengthen thee, help thee, and cause thee to
   stand,
Upheld by my righteous, omnipotent hand.

3 "When through the deep waters I call thee to go,
The rivers of woe shall not thee overflow;
For I will be with thee, thy troubles to bless,
And sanctify to thee thy deepest distress.

4 "When through fiery trials thy pathway shall lie,
   My grace, all-sufficient, shall be thy supply;
   The flame shall not hurt thee; I only design
   Thy dross to consume, and thy gold to refine.

5 "The soul that to Jesus hath fled for repose,
   I will not, I will not desert to his foes;
   That soul, though all hell shall endeavor to shake,
   I'll never, no, never, no, never forsake." Amen.

## 11. (29)

1 In the cross of Christ I glory,
     Towering o'er the wrecks of time;
   All the light of sacred story
     Gathers round its head sublime.

2 When the woes of life o'ertake me,
     Hopes deceive, and fears annoy,
   Never shall the cross forsake me:
     Lo! it glows with peace and joy.

3 When the sun of bliss is beaming
     Light and love upon my way,
   From the cross the radiance streaming,
     Adds new luster to the day.

4 Bane and blessing, pain and pleasure,
     By the cross are sanctified;
   Peace is there that knows no measure,
     Joys that through all time abide.

5 In the cross of Christ I glory,
     Towering o'er the wrecks of time;
   All the light of sacred story
     Gathers round its head sublime. Amen.

**12.**     (30)

1 When I survey the wondrous cross
   On which the Prince of glory died,
My richest gain I count but loss,
   And pour contempt on all my pride.

2 Forbid it, Lord, that I should boast,
   Save in the cross of Christ, my God:
All the vain things that charm me most,
   I sacrifice them to his blood.

3 See, from His head, His hands, His feet,
   Sorrow and love flow mingled down!
Did e'er such love and sorrow meet,
   Or thorns compose so rich a crown?

4 Were the whole realm of nature mine,
   That were a tribute far too small;
Love so amazing, so divine,
   Demands my soul, my life, my all. Amen.

**13.**     (33)

1 Jesus Christ is ris'n today,
       Alleluia!
Our triumphant holy day,
       Alleluia!
Who did once upon the Cross,
       Alleluia!
Suffer to redeem our loss.
       Alleluia!

2 Hymns of praise then let us sing
Unto Christ, our heavenly King,
Who endured the Cross and grave,
Sinners to redeem and save.
       Alleluia!

3 But the pains which He endured,
   Our salvation have procured;
   Now above the sky He's King,
   Where the angels ever sing.
                              Alleluia!

4 Sing we to our God above
   Praise eternal as His love;
   Praise Him all ye heavenly host,
   Father, Son, and Holy Ghost.
                              Alleluia! Amen.

**14.** (34)

1 The strife is o'er, the battle done,
   The victory of life is won;
   The song of triumph has begun.
                              Alleluia!

2 The powers of death have done their worst,
   But Christ their legions hath dispersed:
   Let shout of holy joy outburst.
                              Alleluia!

3 The three sad days are quickly sped,
   He rises glorious from the dead:
   All glory to our risen Head!
                              Alleluia!

4 He closed the yawning gates of hell,
   The bars from heaven's high portals fell;
   Let hymns of praise his triumphs tell!
                              Alleluia!

5 Lord! by the stripes which wounded Thee,
   From death's dread sting Thy servants free,
   That we may live and sing to Thee.
                              Alleluia! Amen.

**15.**      (35)

1 Peace in our time, O Lord,
  To all the peoples—Peace!
  Peace surely based upon Thy Will
  And built in righteousness.
      Thy power alone can break
      The fetters that enchain
      The sorely-stricken soul of life,
      And make it live again.

2 Too long mistrust and fear
  Have held our souls in thrall;
  Sweep through the earth, keen breath of heaven,
  And sound a nobler call!
      Come, as Thou didst of old,
      In love so great that men
      Shall cast aside all other gods,
      And turn to Thee again!

3 O, shall we never learn
  The truth all time has taught,—
  That without God as architect
  Our building comes to naught?
      Lord, help us, and inspire
      Our hearts and lives, that we
      May build, with all Thy wondrous gifts,
      A Kingdom meet for Thee.

4 Peace in our time, O Lord,
  To all the peoples—Peace!
  Peace that shall crown a glad new world,
  And make for life's increase.
      O Living Christ, who still
      Dost all our burdens share,
      Come now and reign within the hearts
      Of all men everywhere!

**16.**    (28)

1 Just as I am, without one plea,
   But that Thy blood was shed for me,
   And that Thou bidd'st me come to Thee,
   O Lamb of God, I come, I come.

2 Just as I am, and waiting not
   To rid my soul of one dark blot,
   To Thee, Whose blood can cleanse each spot,
   O Lamb of God, I come.

3 Just as I am, though tossed about
   With many a conflict, many a doubt,
   Fightings and fears within, without,
   O Lamb of God, I come.

4 Just as I am, poor, wretched, blind;
   Sight, riches, healing of the mind,
   Yea, all I need, in Thee to find,
   O Lamb of God, I come.

5 Just as I am: Thou wilt receive,
   Wilt welcome, pardon, cleanse, relieve,
   Because Thy promise I believe,
   O Lamb of God, I come.

6 Just as I am, Thy love unknown
   Has broken every barrier down;
   Now to be Thine, yea, Thine alone,
   O Lamb of God, I come. Amen.

**17.**    (39)

1 Holy, Holy, Holy! Lord God Almighty!
   Early in the morning our song shall rise to Thee:
Holy, Holy, Holy! merciful and mighty!
   God in Three Persons, blessed Trinity.

2 Holy, Holy, Holy! All the saints adore Thee,
    Casting down their golden crowns around the
        glassy sea;
Cherubim and seraphim falling down before Thee,
    Which wert, and art, and evermore shalt be.

3 Holy, Holy, Holy! though the darkness hide Thee,
    Though the eye of sinful man Thy glory may not
        see,
Only Thou art holy; there is none beside Thee,
    Perfect in power, in love, and purity.

4 Holy, Holy, Holy! Lord God Almighty!
    All Thy works shall praise Thy Name, in earth,
        and sky, and sea;
Holy, Holy, Holy! merciful and mighty!
    God in Three Persons, blessed Trinity. Amen.

**18.**              (41)

1 Blest be the tie that binds
    Our hearts in Jesus' love:
The fellowship of Christian minds
    Is like to that above.

2 Before our Father's throne
    We pour united prayers;
Our fears, our hopes, our aims are one;
    Our comforts and our cares.

3 We share our mutual woes,
    Our mutual burdens bear;
And often for each other flows
    The sympathizing tear.

4 When we at death must part,
    Not like the world's, our pain;
But one in Christ, and one in heart,
    We part to meet again.

5 From sorrow, toil, and pain,
    And sin, we shall be free;
And perfect love and friendship reign
    Throughout eternity. Amen.

**19.**              (42)

1 My faith looks up to thee,
    Thou Lamb of Calvary,
      Saviour divine!
Now hear me while I pray;
Take all my guilt away;
O let me from this day
      Be wholly thine.

2 May thy rich grace impart
    Strength to my fainting heart,
      My zeal inspire;
As thou hast died for me,
O may my love to thee
Pure, warm, and changeless be,
      A living fire.

3 While life's dark maze I tread,
    And griefs around me spread,
      Be thou my guide;
Bid darkness turn to day;
Wipe sorrow's tears away;
Nor let me ever stray
      From thee aside!

4 When ends life's transient dream,
   When death's cold, sullen stream
     Shall o'er me roll;
   Blest Saviour, then in love,
   Fear and distrust remove;
   O bear me safe above,
     A ransomed soul! Amen.

**20.**          **(43)**

1 All hail the power of Jesus' Name!
   Let angels prostrate fall;
   Bring forth the royal diadem,
   And crown him Lord of all!

2 Crown him, ye martyrs of our God,
   Who from his altar call:
   Extol the Stem-of-Jesse's rod,
   And crown him Lord of all!

3 Hail him, the Heir of David's line,
   Whom David, Lord did call;
   The God incarnate! Man divine!
   And crown him Lord of all!

4 Ye seed of Israel's chosen race,
   Ye ransomed of the fall,
   Hail him who saves you by his grace,
   And crown him Lord of all!

5 Sinners, whose love can ne'er forget
   The wormwood and the gall,
   Go, spread your trophies at his feet,
   And crown him Lord of all!

6 Let every kindred, every tribe,
    Before him prostrate fall!
To him all majesty ascribe,
    And crown him Lord of all! Amen.

**21.** (44)

1 God moves in a mysterious way
    His wonders to perform;
He plants His footsteps in the sea,
    And rides upon the storm.

2 Deep in unfathomable mines,
    With never failing skill,
He treasures up His bright designs,
    And works His sovereign will.

3 Ye fearful saints, fresh courage take;
    The clouds ye so much dread
Are big with mercy, and shall break
    In blessings on your head.

4 Judge not the Lord by feeble sense,
    But trust Him for His grace;
Behind a frowning providence
    He hides a smiling face.

5 His purposes will ripen fast,
    Unfolding every hour;
The bud may have a bitter taste,
    But sweet will be the flower.

6 Blind unbelief is sure to err,
    And scan His work in vain;
God is His own interpreter,
    And He will make it plain. Amen.

**22.** (45)

1 Rock of ages, cleft for me,
Let me hide myself in thee;
Let the water and the blood
From thy side, a healing flood,
Be of sin the double cure,
Save from wrath, and make me pure.

2 Should my tears for ever flow,
Should my zeal no languor know,
All for sin could not atone,
Thou must save, and thou alone;
In my hand no price I bring,
Simply to thy cross I cling.

3 While I draw this fleeting breath,
When mine eyelids close in death,
When I rise to worlds unknown,
And behold thee on thy throne,
Rock of ages, cleft for me,
Let me hide myself in thee. Amen.

**23.** (47)

1 Jesus, Lover of my soul,
Let me to thy bosom fly,
While the nearer waters roll,
While the tempest still is high:
Hide me, O my Saviour, hide,
Till the storm of life be past;
Safe into the haven guide,
O receive my soul at last!

2 Other refuge have I none,
    Hangs my helpless soul on thee;
Leave, ah! leave me not alone,
    Still support and comfort me!
All my trust on thee is stayed;
    All my help from thee I bring;
Cover my defenceless head
    With the shadow of thy wing.

3 Plenteous grace with thee is found,
    Grace to cleanse from every sin;
Let the healing streams abound,
    Make and keep me pure within.
Thou of life the fountain art,
    Freely let me take of thee:
Spring thou up within my heart,
    Rise to all eternity. Amen.

**24.**                                    (48)

1 O Love that wilt not let me go,
    I rest my weary soul in thee;
I give thee back the life I owe,
That in thine ocean depths its flow
    May richer, fuller be.

2 O Light that followest all my way,
    I yield my flickering torch to thee;
My heart restores its borrowed ray,
That in thy sunshine's blaze its day
    May brighter, fairer be.

3 O Joy that seekest me through pain,
    I cannot close my heart to thee;
I trace the rainbow through the rain,
And feel the promise is not vain
    That morn shall tearless be.

4 O Cross that liftest up my head,
    I dare not ask to fly from thee;
I lay in dust life's glory dead,
And from the ground there blossoms red
    Life that shall endless be. Amen.

**25.**          (51)

1 There's a wideness in God's mercy
    Like the wideness of the sea;
There's a kindness in his justice,
    Which is more than liberty.
There is welcome for the sinner,
    And more graces for the good;
There is mercy with the Saviour;
    There is healing in his blood.

2 There is no place where earth's sorrows
    Are more felt than up in heaven;
There is no place where earth's failings
    Have such kindly judgment given.
There is plentiful redemption
    In the blood that has been shed;
There is joy for all the members
    In the sorrows of the Head.

3 For the love of God is broader
    Than the measure of man's mind;
And the heart of the Eternal
    Is most infinitely kind.
If our love were but more simple,
    We should take him at his word;
And our lives would be all sunshine
    In the sweetness of the Lord.

**26.** (54)

1 For all the saints who from their labors rest,
Who Thee by faith before the world confessed,
Thy name, O Jesus, be forever blest,
Alleluia! Alleluia!

2 Thou wast their Rock, their Fortress, and their Might;
Thou, Lord, their Captain in the well-fought fight;
Thou, in the darkness drear, their own true Light.
Alleluia!

3 O may Thy soldiers, faithful, true, and bold,
Fight as the saints who nobly fought of old,
And win with them the victor's crown of gold.
Alleluia!

4 O blest communion, fellowship divine!
We feebly struggle, they in glory shine;
Yet all are one in Thee, for all are Thine.
Alleluia!

5 And when the strife is fierce, the warfare long,
Steals on the ear the distant triumph song,
And hearts are brave again, and arms are strong.
Alleluia!

6 The golden evening brightens in the west;
Soon, soon to faithful warriors cometh rest;
Sweet is the calm of Paradise the blest.
Alleluia!

7 From earth's wide bounds, from ocean's farthest coast,
Through gates of pearl streams in the countless host,
Singing to Father, Son and Holy Ghost.
Alleluia! Amen.

**27.**     (55)

1 I love Thy kingdom, Lord,
    The house of Thine abode,
The Church our blest Redeemer saved
    With His own precious blood.

2 For her my tears shall fall;
    For her my prayers ascend;
To her my cares and toils be given,
    Till toils and cares shall end.

3 Beyond my highest joy
    I prize her heavenly ways,
Her sweet communion, solemn vows,
    Her hymns of love and praise.

4 Jesus, Thou Friend divine,
    Our Saviour and our King,
Thy hand from every snare and foe
    Shall great deliverance bring.

5 Sure as Thy truth shall last,
    To Sion shall be given
The brightest glories earth can yield,
    And brighter bliss of heaven. Amen.

**28.**     (60)

1 Jesus calls us; o'er the tumult
    Of our life's wild, restless sea,
Day by day His sweet voice soundeth,
    Saying, "Christian, follow Me."

2 As of old, Saint Andrew heard it
    By the Galilean lake,
Turned from home, and toil, and kindred,
    Leaving all for His dear sake.

3 Jesus calls us from the worship
    Of the vain world's golden store;
  From each idol that would keep us,
    Saying, "Christian, love Me more."

4 In our joys and in our sorrows,
    Days of toil and hours of ease,
  Still He calls, in cares and pleasures,
    "That we love Him more than these."

5 Jesus calls us: by Thy mercies,
    Saviour, make us hear Thy call,
  Give our hearts to Thine obedience,
    Serve and love Thee best of all. Amen.

**29.** (62)

1 Eternal Father! strong to save,
  Whose arm hath bound the restless wave,
  Who bidd'st the mighty ocean deep
  Its own appointed limits keep:
    O hear us when we cry to Thee
    For those in peril on the sea!

2 O Christ! whose voice the waters heard
  And hushed their raging at Thy word,
  Who walkedst on the foaming deep,
  And calm amidst its rage didst sleep;
    O hear us when we cry to Thee
    For those in peril on the sea!

3 Most Holy Spirit! who didst brood
  Upon the chaos dark and rude,
  And bid its angry tumult cease,
  And give, for wild confusion, peace;
    O hear us when we cry to Thee
    For those in peril on the sea!

4 O Trinity of love and power
  Our brethren shield in danger's hour;
From rock and tempest, fire and foe,
Protect them wheresoe'er they go;
    Thus evermore shall rise to Thee
Glad hymns of praise from land and sea. Amen.

**30.** (63)

1 Now thank we all our God,
    With heart, and hands, and voices!
Who wondrous things hath done,
    In whom His world rejoices;
Who from our mother's arms
    Hath blessed us on our way
With countless gifts of love;
    And still is ours to-day.

2 O may this bounteous God
    Through all our life be near us!
With ever-joyful hearts
    And blessèd peace to cheer us;
And keep us in His grace,
    And guide us when perplext;
And free us from all ills
    In this world and the next. Amen.

**31.** (65)

1 O beautiful for spacious skies,
    For amber waves of grain,
For purple mountain majesties
    Above the fruited plain!
America! America!
    God shed His grace on thee,
And crown thy good with brotherhood
    From sea to shining sea.

2 O beautiful for pilgrim feet,
  Whose stern, impassioned stress
A thoroughfare for freedom beat
  Across the wilderness!
America! America!
  God mend thine every flaw,
Confirm thy soul in self control,
  Thy liberty in law.

3 O beautiful for heroes proved
  In liberating strife,
Who more than self their country loved,
  And mercy more than life!
America! America!
  May God thy gold refine,
Till all success be nobleness,
  And every gain divine.

4 O beautiful for patriot dream
  That sees, beyond the years,
Thine alabaster cities gleam,
  Undimmed by human tears!
America! America!
  God shed His grace on thee
And crown thy good with brotherhood
  From sea to shining sea. Amen.

**32.**                    (68)

1 God bless our native land;
  Firm may she ever stand
    Through storm and night:
  When the wild tempests rave,
  Ruler of wind and wave,
  Do Thou our country save
    By Thy great might.

2 For her our prayers shall rise
   To God above the skies;
     On Him we wait;
   Thou who art ever nigh,
   Guarding with watchful eye,
   To Thee aloud we cry,
     God save the state!

3 Our fathers' God, to Thee,
   Author of liberty,
     To Thee we sing:
   Long may our land be bright
   With freedom's holy light;
   Protect us by Thy might,
     Great God, our King. Amen.

**33.**                **(68)**

1 My country, 'tis of thee,
   Sweet land of liberty,
     Of thee I sing;
   Land where my fathers died,
   Land of the pilgrims' pride,
   From every mountainside
     Let freedom ring.

2 My native country, thee,
   Land of the noble free,
     Thy name I love;
   I love thy rocks and rills,
   Thy woods and templed hills;
   My heart with rapture thrills
     Like that above.

3 Let music swell the breeze,
   And ring from all the trees
     Sweet freedom's song;
   Let mortal tongues awake,
   Let all that breathe partake,
   Let rocks their silence break,
     The sound prolong.

4 Our fathers' God, to thee,
   Author of liberty,
     To thee we sing;
   Long may our land be bright
   With freedom's holy light;
   Protect us by thy might,
     Great God, our King. Amen.

**34.**                     **(71)**

1 Once to every man and nation
   Comes the moment to decide,
In the strife of truth with falsehood,
   For the good or evil side;
Some great cause, God's new Messiah,
   Offering each the bloom or blight,
And the choice goes by for ever
   'Twixt that darkness and that light.

2 Then to side with truth is noble,
   When we share her wretched crust,
Ere her cause bring fame and profit,
   And 'tis prosperous to be just;
Then it is the brave man chooses,
   While the coward stands aside
Till the multitude make virtue
   Of the faith they had denied.

3 By the light of burning martyrs
    Jesus' bleeding feet I track,
Toiling up new Calvaries ever
    With the cross that turns not back;
New occasions teach new duties,
    Time makes ancient good uncouth;
They must upward still and onward,
    Who would keep abreast of truth.

4 Though the cause of evil prosper,
    Yet 'tis truth alone is strong;
Though her portion be the scaffold,
    And upon the throne be wrong,
Yet that scaffold sways the future,
    And, behind the dim unknown,
Standeth God within the shadow
    Keeping watch above his own. Amen.

**5.** (74)

1 The Church's one foundation
    Is Jesus Christ her Lord;
She is his new creation
    By water and the word:
From heaven he came and sought her
    To be his holy bride;
With his own blood he bought her,
    And for her life he died.

2 Elect from every nation,
    Yet one o'er all the earth,
Her charter of salvation,
    One Lord, one faith, one birth;
One holy Name she blesses,
    Partakes one holy food,
And to one hope she presses,
    With every grace endued.

3 Though with a scornful wonder
    Men see her sore opprest,
By schisms rent asunder,
    By heresies distrest;
Yet saints their watch are keeping,
    Their cry goes up, "How long?"
And soon the night of weeping
    Shall be the morn of song.

4 'Mid toil and tribulation,
    And tumult of her war,
She waits the consummation
    Of peace for evermore;
Till with the vision glorious
    Her longing eyes are blest,
And the great Church victorious
    Shall be the Church at rest.

5 Yet she on earth hath union
    With God the Three in One,
And mystic sweet communion
    With those whose rest is won.
O happy ones and holy!
    Lord, give us grace that we
Like them, the meek and lowly,
    On high may dwell with thee. Amen.

**36.** (75)

1 Glorious things of thee are spoken,
    Sion, city of our God;
He whose word cannot be broken,
    Formed thee for his own abode;
On the Rock of Ages founded,
    What can shake thy sure repose?
With salvation's walls surrounded,
    Thou may'st smile at all thy foes.

2 See, the streams of living waters
Springing from eternal love,
Well supply thy sons and daughters,
And all fear of want remove.
Who can faint, when such a river
Ever will their thirst assuage?
Grace which, like the Lord, the giver,
Never fails from age to age.

3 Round each habitation hovering,
See the cloud and fire appear
For a glory and a covering,
Showing that the Lord is near.
Thus deriving from their banner,
Light by night, and shade by day,
Safe they feed upon the manna,
Which he gives them when they pray.

4 Blest inhabitants of Sion,
Washed in the Redeemer's blood!
Jesus, whom their souls rely on,
Makes them kings and priests to God.
'Tis his love his people raises
Over self to reign as kings:
And as priests, his solemn praises
Each for a thank-offering brings. Amen.

**37.** (76)

1 Jesus shall reign where'er the sun
Doth his successive journeys run;
His kingdom stretch from shore to shore,
Till moons shall wax and wane no more.

2 To him shall endless prayer be made,
And praises throng to crown his head;
His Name like sweet perfume shall rise
With every morning sacrifice.

3 People and realms of every tongue
   Dwell on his love with sweetest song;
   And infant voices shall proclaim
   Their early blessings on his Name.

4 Blessings abound where'er he reigns;
   The prisoner leaps to lose his chains,
   The weary find eternal rest,
   And all the sons of want are blest.

5 Let every creature rise and bring
   Peculiar honors to our King;
   Angels descend with songs again,
   And earth repeat the loud Amen.

**38.**　　　　　(79)

1 Rise up, O men of God!
   Have done with lesser things,
   Give heart, and soul, and mind, and strength
   To serve the King of kings.

2 Rise up, O men of God!
   His kingdom tarries long.
   Bring in the day of brotherhood
   And end the night of wrong.

3 Lift high the cross of Christ!
   Tread where His feet have trod.
   As brothers of the Son of man,
   Rise up, O men of God! Amen.

**39.**　　　　　(80)

1 O Master, let me walk with thee
   In lowly paths of service free;
   Tell me thy secret; help me bear
   The strain of toil, the fret of care.

2 Help me the slow of heart to move
By some clear, winning word of love;
Teach me the wayward feet to stay,
And guide them in the homeward way.

3 Teach me thy patience; still with thee
In closer, dearer company,
In work that keeps faith sweet and strong,
In trust that triumphs over wrong.

4 In hope that sends a shining ray
Far down the future's broadening way,
In peace that only thou canst give,
With thee, O Master, let me live. Amen.

**40.** (82)

1 Onward, Christian soldiers
Marching as to war,
With the cross of Jesus
Going on before!
Christ the royal Master,
Leads against the foe;
Forward into battle,
See, his banners go.
Onward, Christian soldiers,
Marching as to war,
With the cross of Jesus
Going on before!

2 At the sign of triumph
Satan's host doth flee;
On, then, Christian soldiers,
On to victory!

Hell's foundations quiver
  At the shout of praise;
Brothers, lift your voices,
  Loud your anthems raise!
    Onward, etc.

3 Like a mighty army
    Moves the Church of God;
Brothers, we are treading
    Where the saints have trod;
We are not divided,
    All one body we,
One in hope and doctrine,
    One in charity.
      Onward, etc.

4 Crowns and thrones may perish,
    Kingdoms rise and wane,
But the Church of Jesus
    Constant will remain;
Gates of hell can never
    'Gainst that Church prevail;
We have Christ's own promise,
    And that cannot fail.
      Onward, etc.

5 Onward, then, ye people!
    Join our happy throng!
Blend with ours your voices
    In the triumph song!
Glory, laud, and honor,
    Unto Christ the King;
This through countless ages
    Men and angels sing.
      Onward, etc.     Amen.

(83)

1 Stand up, stand up, for Jesus,
   Ye soldiers of the cross!
Lift high his royal banner!
   It must not suffer loss:
From victory unto victory
   His army shall he lead;
Till every foe is vanquished,
   And Christ is Lord indeed.

2 Stand up, stand up, for Jesus!
   The trumpet call obey!
Forth to the mighty conflict
   In this his glorious day!
Ye that are men now serve him
   Against unnumbered foes!
Let courage rise with danger,
   And strength to strength oppose.

3 Stand up, stand up, for Jesus!
   Stand in his strength alone!
The arm of flesh will fail you,
   Ye dare not trust your own:
Put on the Gospel armor,
   And watching unto prayer,
When duty calls, or danger,
   Be never wanting there!

4 Stand up, stand up, for Jesus!
   The strife will not be long:
This day, the noise of battle;
   The next, the victor's song.
To him that overcometh,
   A crown of life shall be;
He with the King of glory
   Shall reign eternally. Amen.

**42.** (85)

1 Be still, my soul: the Lord is on thy side;
    Bear patiently the cross of grief or pain;
Leave to thy God to order and provide;
    In every change he faithful will remain.
Be still, my soul: thy best, thy heavenly Friend
Thro' thorny ways leads to a joyful end.

2 Be still, my soul: thy God doth undertake
    To guide the future as he has the past.
Thy hope, thy confidence let nothing shake;
    All now mysterious shall be bright at last.
Be still, my soul: the waves and winds still know
His voice who ruled them while he dwelt below.

3 Be still, my soul: the hour is hastening on
    When we shall be forever with the Lord,
When disappointment, grief, and fear are gone,
    Sorrow forgot, love's purest joys restored.
Be still, my soul: when change and tears are past,
All safe and blessed we shall meet at last. Amen.

**43.** (89)

1 We gather together to ask the Lord's blessing;
    He chastens and hastens his will to make known;
The wicked oppressing now cease from distressing,
    Sing praises to his Name; he forgets not his own.

2 Beside us to guide us, our God with us joining,
    Ordaining, maintaining his kingdom divine;
So from the beginning the fight we were winning:
    Thou, Lord, wast at our side, all glory be thine!

3 We all do extol thee, thou leader triumphant,
　　And pray that thou still our defender wilt be.
Let thy congregation escape tribulation:
　　Thy Name be ever praised! O Lord, make us free!
　　　　　　　　　　　　　　　　　Amen.

**44.**　　　　　　　　　(91)

1 O God, our help in ages past,
　　Our hope for years to come,
　　Our shelter from the stormy blast
　　And our eternal home:

2 Under the shadow of thy throne
　　Thy saints have dwelt secure;
　　Sufficient is thine arm alone,
　　And our defence is sure.

3 Before the hills in order stood,
　　Or earth received her frame,
　　From everlasting thou art God,
　　To endless years the same.

4 A thousand ages in thy sight
　　Are like an evening gone;
　　Short as the watch that ends the night
　　Before the rising sun.

5 Time, like an ever-rolling stream,
　　Bears all its sons away;
　　They fly, forgotten, as a dream
　　Dies at the opening day.

6 O God, our help in ages past,
　　Our hope for years to come,
　　Be thou our guide while life shall last
　　And our eternal home. Amen.

**45.**

1 Mine eyes have seen the glory of the coming of the
  Lord;
  He is trampling out the vintage where the grapes
    of wrath are stored;
  He hath loosed the fateful lightning of His terrible
    swift sword;
  His truth is marching on.

(Refrain)

*Glory! glory! Hallelujah!*
*Glory! glory! Hallelujah!*
*Glory! glory! Hallelujah!*
  1. *His truth is marching on.*
  2. *His day is marching on.*
  3. *Since God is marching on.*
  4. *Our God is marching on.*
  5. *While God is marching on.*

2 I have seen Him in the watch-fires of a hundred
  circling camps;
  They have builded Him an altar in the evening
    dews and damps;
  I have read His righteous sentence by the dim and
    flaring lamps:
  His day is marching on. (*Refrain*)

3 I have read a fiery gospel, writ in burnished rows
  of steel:
  "As ye deal with My contemners, so with you My
    grace shall deal;"
  Let the Hero, born of woman, crush the serpent
    with His heel,
  Since God is marching on. (*Refrain*)

4 He has sounded forth His trumpet that shall never
    call retreat;
  He is sifting out the hearts of men before His
    judgment-seat;
  O be swift, my soul, to answer Him: be jubilant,
    my feet!
  Our God is marching on. (*Refrain*)

5 In the beauty of the lilies Christ was born, across
    the sea,
  With a glory in His bosom that transfigures you
    and me;
  As He died to make men holy, let us die to make
    men free!
  While God is marching on. (*Refrain*) Amen.

**46.**             (57)

1 The King of love my Shepherd is,
    Whose goodness faileth never:
  I nothing lack if I am His,
    And He is mine for ever.

2 Where streams of living water flow
    My ransomed soul He leadeth,
  And where the verdant pastures grow,
    With food celestial feedeth.

3 Perverse and foolish oft I strayed,
    But yet in love He sought me,
  And on His shoulder gently laid,
    And home, rejoicing, brought me.

4 In death's dark vale I fear no ill
    With Thee, dear Lord, beside me;
  Thy rod and staff my comfort still,
    Thy Cross before to guide me.

5 Thou spread'st a table in my sight;
   Thy unction grace bestoweth;
   And O what transport of delight
   From Thy pure chalice floweth!

6 And so through all the length of days,
   Thy goodness faileth never;
   Good Shepherd, may I sing Thy praise
   Within Thy house for ever.   Amen.

Acknowledgment is due the Forward Movement Publications, 412 Sycamore Street, Cincinnati, Ohio, who have kindly granted permission to include in this volume the following: Baptism in Extremis from "Manual For Servicemen", A form of Confession from "Be of Good Cheer", prayer For a Day of Battle from "God Be With You", prayers For Our Armed Forces and For Chaplains in the Armed Forces from "Prayers for All Occasions", prayers For A Will to Peace, For the Bereaved, For the United Nations, For Courage, For our Enemies from "War-Time Prayers". The services of Holy Communion and The Ministration of Holy Baptism are taken from The Book of Common Prayer.

# Index of Hymns

Numbers in parentheses indicate the numbers of the hymns in The Wayside Hymnal, published by The Forward Movement, Cincinnati 2, Ohio.

# Index of Prayers

# The Star-Spangled Banner

O say can you see, by the dawn's early light,
What so proudly we hailed at the twilight's last
gleaming,
Whose broad stripes and bright stars, through the
perilous fight,
O'er the ramparts we watched, were so gallantly
streaming?
And the rockets' red glare, the bombs bursting in air,
Gave proof through the night that our flag was still
there.
O say does that star-spangled banner yet wave
O'er the land of the free and the home of the brave?

## 2

O thus be it ever, when freemen shall stand
Between their loved homes and the war's desolation!
Blest with vict'ry and peace, may the heav'n-rescued
land
Praise the Power that hath made and preserved us a
nation!
Then conquer we must, when our cause it is just,
And this be our motto, "In God is our trust."
And the star-spangled banner in triumph shall wave
O'er the land of the free and the home of the brave!